CONTENT WRITER

A COMPLETE GUIDE FOR
CONTENT WRITER

BY
BILAL MOAWIA AULAKH

1

Copyright

Disclaimer

The information contained in this ebook is for general informational purposes only. It is not intended to be a substitute for professional advice on becoming a content writer. While the information in this ebook was believed to be accurate at the time of publication, the field of content writing is constantly evolving. Therefore the information contained in this ebook may be outdated or incorrect. The author and publisher of this ebook make no representations or warranties of any kind, express or implied, about the completeness, accuracy, reliability,

Contents

Introduction of the content write

A content writer is a professional writer who creates written content for a variety of platforms and audiences. Content writers may create content for websites, blogs, social media, marketing materials, and other types of online or offline media.

Content writers are responsible for researching, writing, and editing content that is engaging, informative, and relevant to the intended audience. They may work with clients or businesses to create content that meets specific goals or objectives, such as increasing website traffic or promoting a product or service.

Content writers may specialize in a specific industry or subject area, such as healthcare, technology, or travel. They may also have expertise in a particular type of content, such as SEO writing, technical writing, or creative writing.

Content writing is a growing field, with many businesses and organizations seeking professional writers to create content for their websites, social media, and marketing materials. Content writers may work as freelancers, for a content writing agency, or in-house for a company or organization.

Overall, content writing is a rewarding profession that allows writers to share their knowledge and expertise with a wide audience, while also helping businesses and organizations achieve their marketing and communication goals.

History of the content writer

The concept of content writing has a long history, dating back to the earliest forms of written communication. However, the modern concept of content writing as we know it today emerged with the advent of the internet and the proliferation of online content.

In the early days of the internet, content writing was primarily focused on creating written content for websites. As the internet and online content grew in popularity, businesses and organizations began to see the value in creating high-quality, engaging content for their websites and marketing materials.

In the late 1990s and early 2000s, the field of content writing began to evolve and professional content writers emerged as a new type of content creator. With the proliferation of social media and the rise of content marketing, the demand for professional content writers continued to grow.

Today, content writing is a multi-billion dollar industry, with content writers creating written content for a wide variety of platforms and audiences. From websites and blogs to social media and marketing materials, content writers play a crucial role in helping businesses and organizations communicate with their audience and achieve their marketing and communication goals.

The importance of content writing:
Content writing is an important part of the online landscape and has many benefits for businesses, organizations, and society as a whole. Some of the key benefits of content writing include:

Improved communication: Good content writing helps businesses and organizations communicate more effectively with their audience. By creating well-written, engaging content, content writers can help business and organizations convey their message clearly and effectively.

Increased website traffic: High-quality content can help businesses and organizations attract and retain website visitors, leading to increased traffic and engagement.

Enhanced search engine optimization (SEO): By using keywords and other SEO techniques, content writers can help businesses and organizations improve their search engine rankings and increase the visibility of their websites.

Establishing authority and credibility: By consistently creating high-quality content, businesses and organizations can establish themselves as thought leaders in their industry and build credibility with their audience.

Increased conversions and sales: Good content writing can help businesses and organizations convert website visitors into customers, leading to increased sales and revenue.

Overall, content writing is an important part of the online landscape and offers many benefits for businesses, organizations, and society as a whole. It is a crucial tool for effective communication and can help businesses and organizations attract and retain website visitors, improve their search engine rankings, and increase conversions and sales.

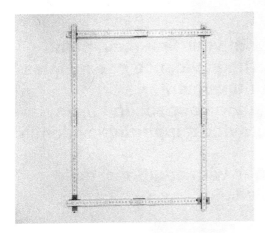

An outline for a content writer:

Here is an outline that a content writer could use when creating an article or blog post:

Introduction

Hook: Start with a hook to grab the reader's attention and make them want to keep reading.
Background: Provide some background information on the topic you will be discussing.
Thesis: Clearly state the main point or purpose of your article.

II. Body
Point 1: Start with your first main point. Provide supporting evidence or examples to back up your argument.
Point 2: Move on to your second main point. Again, provide supporting evidence or examples.
Point 3: Continue with additional main points as needed.

III. Conclusion
Summarize your main points and restate your thesis.
End with a call to action, encouraging the reader to take some action or leave a comment.
Remember to keep your outline flexible and adjust it as needed as you write. It can also be helpful to include sub-points under

each main point to provide additional structure and detail.
 Write a good hook to grab your reader's attention.

Role of hooking wording in writing:
A hook, also known as a lead or an attention-grabber, is a word or phrase that is used at the beginning of a piece of writing to grab the reader's attention and encourage them to keep reading. The role of a hook is to engage the reader and make them want to learn more about the topic or content being presented.

There are many different types of hooks that writers can use, depending on the tone and style of their writing and the audience they are targeting. Some common types of hooks include

A question: Asking a thought-provoking or intriguing question can grab the reader's attention and make them want to find out the answer.

A quote: Including a quote from a well-known or influential person can add credibility and interest to your content.

A statistic: Using a surprising or relevant statistic can help to illustrate the importance or relevance of your topic.

A story: Telling a story or anecdote can help to engage the reader and make your content more relatable.

A description: Describing a person, place, or thing in vivid or sensory language can help to draw the reader in and create a sense of curiosity or intrigue.

Regardless of the type of hook you choose, it's important to make sure it is relevant and appropriate for your content and audience. A good hook should be compelling and draw the reader in, but it should also be authentic and genuine, and not feel forced or artificial.

Here are a few examples of hooks that could be used to grab a reader's attention:

A shocking statistic or fact: "Did you know that over 50% of all marriages end in divorce?"

A provocative or thought-provoking question: "Have you ever stopped to consider the impact of social media on our relationships?"

An intriguing anecdote or story: "As I stood on the edge of the cliff, I couldn't help but wonder how I had gotten myself into this situation."

A strong statement or opinion: "It's time we put an end to the myth that beauty is only skin deep."

A rhetorical question: "Who wouldn't want to live in a world where everyone is treated with kindness and respect?"

Remember, the goal of a hook is to grab the reader's attention and make them want to keep reading. Choose a hook that fits with the tone and subject matter of your article and use it to draw the reader in.

What is a content writer?
A content writer is a professional writer who creates written content for a variety of

purposes, such as websites, blogs, social media, marketing materials, and more. Content writers may specialize in a particular type of content, such as web copy, articles, or social media posts, or may create a variety of content for different platforms and audiences.

How to become a content writer?
Here are some steps you can follow to become a content writer:

Build your writing skills: To become a content writer, it's important to have strong writing skills. You can improve your writing skills by reading and writing regularly, taking writing courses or workshops, and seeking feedback from others.

Develop your niche: Content writers often specialize in a specific niche or industry, such as technology, healthcare, or marketing. Consider developing your expertise in a particular area to make you more attractive to potential clients.

Create a portfolio: A portfolio is a collection of your writing samples that demonstrates your skills and abilities. You can create a portfolio by writing blog posts, articles, or other types of content and including them in your portfolio.

Learn about SEO: Search engine optimization (SEO) is the practice of optimizing your website or content to rank well in search engine results. As a content writer, it's important to have a basic understanding of SEO to create content that is optimized for search engines.

Learn about content marketing: Content marketing is the practice of creating and distributing valuable, relevant, and consistent content to attract and retain a clearly defined audience. As a content writer, it's important to have a basic understanding of content marketing to create effective content.

Find writing opportunities: There are many opportunities for content writers, including freelance writing, working for a content marketing agency, or working as an in-house writer for a company. Consider applying for writing jobs or pitching your services to potential clients.

Build your network: Building a network of contacts in the writing industry can be helpful in finding writing opportunities and getting your work noticed. Consider joining writing organizations or attending writing conferences to meet other writers and professionals in the industry.

Keep learning: To stay current in the field of content writing, it's important to continue learning and improving your skills. Consider taking writing courses, attending writing conferences, and reading industry publications to stay.

How to create content?
Choose a topic: The first step in creating content is to decide what you want to write about. Choose a topic that is relevant to your audience and fits with your overall content strategy.

Research your topic: Once you have chosen a topic, gather all necessary information and sources to help you write accurately and effectively. This may involve conducting online research, interviewing experts, or reviewing relevant studies or reports.

Create an outline: An outline can help you to organize your ideas and ensure that your content flows logically. Consider dividing your content into sections or using headings and subheadings to help break up the text.

Write your content: Begin writing your content, using your outline as a guide. Focus on using clear and concise language and engaging your readers with interesting and informative content.

Edit and proofread: Review your content for errors in grammar, spelling, punctuation, and style. Consider asking a colleague or friend to review your content for additional feedback.

Add images and other visual elements: Consider adding images, videos, infographics, or other visual elements to your content to make it more engaging and visually appealing.

Optimize for search engines: If you are publishing your content online, consider including relevant keywords and optimizing your content for search engines to improve its visibility in search results.

Publish your content: Once you have finished creating your content, publish it in the appropriate format (e.g., blog post, webpage, social media post).

Promote your content: Consider promoting your content through social media, email marketing, or other channels to help increase its reach and visibility.

Measure and analyze your results: Use tools like Google Analytics to track the performance of your content and identify areas for improvement. This can help you to refine your content creation strategy and create even more effective content in the future.

What are the resources to become a content writer?
Here are some resources that can help you to become a content writer:

Books: There are many books available on content writing, covering topics such as writing for the web, SEO, and content strategy. Some popular books on content writing include "Everybody Writes" by Ann Handley and "The Elements of Content Strategy" by Erin Kissane.

Online courses: There are many online courses available that can help you to learn more about content writing and improve your skills. These courses may cover topics such as writing for different platforms, crafting compelling headlines, and using SEO to improve your content's visibility.

Websites: There are many websites that offer tips and resources for content writers, including blogs, forums, and online communities. These sites can be a great way to stay up to date on industry trends and learn from experienced content writers.

Writing groups and workshops: Joining a writing group or attending a writing workshop can be a great way to get feedback on your writing and connect with other writers. These groups can be found in person or online and may cover a wide range of topics and genres.

Freelance writing jobs: Gaining practical experience as a content writer can be an important step in building your skills and portfolio. Consider applying for freelance writing jobs or internships to get hands-on experience and build your portfolio.

Professional writing organizations: Joining a professional writing organization, such as the American Writers and Artists Inc. (AWAI) or the Content Marketing Institute (CMI), can provide access to resources, networking opportunities, and professional development opportunities for content writers.

What are the responsibilities of a content writer?

The responsibilities of a content writer may vary depending on the specific role and the needs of the employer, but some common responsibilities may include:

Researching and gathering information on a particular topic
Outlining and organizing the content
Writing clear and engaging copy
Editing and proofreading the content to ensure it is error-free and polished
Meeting deadlines and delivering content on time
Collaborating with other team members, such as designers or developers
Staying up to date on industry trends and best practices in content writing

What skills should a content writer have?

Some skills that a content writer should have include:

Strong writing and editing skills

Good research skills

The ability to organize and structure content effectively

Excellent communication and interpersonal skills

The ability to work independently and meet deadlines

Familiarity with SEO best practices

Proficiency with content management systems and other tools, such as Microsoft Word and Google Docs

What are the education and experience requirements for a content writer?

The education and experience requirements for a content writer may vary depending on the specific role and the needs of the employer. In general, a bachelor's degree in a related field, such as English, journalism, or marketing, is preferred. Some employers may also require previous experience in content writing or a portfolio of writing samples.

No, content writing is not dead today. In fact, the demand for high-quality written content is likely to continue to grow as businesses and organizations recognize the importance of effective communication and marketing through written content.

The role of the content writer may evolve over time as new technologies and platforms emerge, but the need for clear, engaging, and informative written content is not likely to disappear. In fact, as the number of online platforms and channels for communication continues to grow, there may be even more opportunities for content writers to create and share their work.

To stay relevant in the field, content writers may need to continuously update their skills and knowledge of best practices and stay abreast of emerging trends and technologies. However, with the right skills and experience, content writers can continue to play a vital role in helping businesses and organizations communicate with their audiences through written content.

What is the career outlook for content writers?
The career outlook for content writers is generally positive, as businesses and organizations continue to recognize the importance of high-quality written content in marketing and communication efforts. According to the U.S. Bureau of Labor,

What does a content writer do?
A content writer's responsibilities may include:

Researching and gathering information on a particular topic or theme
Outlining and organizing the content of a piece
Writing clear, concise, and engaging copy that meets the needs and interests of the target audience
Using appropriate formatting and visual elements to improve readability and engagement
Proofreading and editing the content to ensure it is error-free and polished

Collaborating with other members of a team or clients to develop content ideas and strategies
Keeping up to date with industry trends and best practices in content creation
What skills are important for a content writer to have?
Some important skills for a content writer to have include:
Excellent writing and editing skills
Strong research and analytical skills
Excellent communication skills
The ability to write in a clear, concise, and engaging style
Proficiency in using formatting and visual elements to improve readability and engagement
Knowledge of SEO principles and how to optimize content for search engines
Familiarity with content management systems and web publishing tools
How do I become a content writer?
To become a content writer, you may need to have a strong background in writing and editing, as well as excellent communication and research skills. Some content writers may have a degree in journalism, English, or a related field, while others may have experience in a particular industry or subject matter that they can draw upon for their writing. Many content

writers also hone their skills through practice and by taking online courses or workshops.

What is the job market like for content writers?

The demand for content writers has grown in recent years due to the increasing importance of content marketing and the proliferation of digital platforms. Many companies and organizations hire content writers to create website copy, blog posts, social media posts, and other written content to promote their products, services, or brand. Freelance content writers may also have the opportunity to work with a variety of clients on a contract basis.

What is the salary range for a content writer?

The salary range for a content writer can vary depending on factors such as the writer's level of experience, the type of content they specialize in, and the location and industry in which they work. According to data from the Bureau of Labor Statistics, the median annual wage for writers and authors in the United States was $62,170 in May 2020. Freelance content writers may earn more or less depending on the rate they charge for their services and the number of clients they work with.

What is the meaning of content writing? Content writing refers to the creation of written content for websites, blogs, social media, and other online platforms. It involves researching and writing articles, blog posts, product descriptions, and other types of written content that are intended to inform, educate, or engage an audience. Content writing aims to provide valuable, relevant, and consistent content that helps to attract and retain a specific target audience. It is an important aspect of digital marketing and can help to increase website traffic, generate leads, and build brand awareness.

Who is called a content writer?
A content writer is a professional writer who creates written content for websites, blogs, social media, and other online platforms. Content writers research and write articles, blog posts, product descriptions, and other types of written content that is intended to inform, educate, or engage an audience. Content writers may work as freelancers, or they may be employed by a company or agency. Their work may be focused on a specific niche

or industry, or they may write about a wide range of topics. The main goal of a content writer is to create engaging and informative content that meets the needs and goals of their clients or employers.

Benefits of a content writer:

Here are 30 benefits of being a content writer:

Flexibility: Many content writers work on a freelance basis, which allows them to set their own schedules and work from anywhere.

Variety: Content writers may have the opportunity to write about a wide range of topics, which can be both challenging and rewarding.

Creative outlet: Content writing allows writers to express their creativity and share their ideas with others.

Professional development: Content writing can be a great way for writers to build their skills and knowledge, as well as their portfolios.

Competitive pay: Some content writers are able to earn a good income from their work.

Opportunity to work with a variety of clients: Content writers may have the opportunity to work with a wide range of clients and industries, which can be exciting and rewarding.

Ability to work remotely: Many content writers work remotely, which allows them to work from home or any location with an internet connection.

Independence: Content writers who work on a freelance basis have the freedom to set their own schedules and work independently.

Ability to learn and grow: Content writing provides the opportunity to learn about new topics and industries, as well as to improve your writing skills.

Impact: Content writers have the ability to reach and influence a wide audience through their writing.

Ability to work on multiple projects at once: Content writers may have the opportunity to work on multiple projects at once, which can be a great way to diversify your income and skills.

Ability to work with a team: Many content writers work with a team of editors, designers, and other professionals, which can be a great way to learn and grow as a writer.

Ability to work on a variety of content formats: Content writers may have the opportunity to write for a variety of content formats, including articles, blog posts, product descriptions, and more.

Ability to work in different industries: Content writers may have the opportunity to work

How many types of content writers?

There are several types of content writers, including

Technical writers: Technical writers create content that explains complex or technical information in a clear and concise way. They may write user manuals, product descriptions, and other types of technical documentation.

Copywriters: Copywriters create persuasive and compelling written content with the goal of selling a product or service. They may write ads, sales letters, and email campaigns.

Blog writers: Blog writers create content for websites or blogs. They may write articles, how-to guides, and other types of content that are intended to inform, educate, or engage an audience.

Social media writers: Social media writers create content for social media platforms, such as Facebook, Twitter, and Instagram. They may write posts, tweets, and captions that are intended to engage followers and promote products or services.

Ghostwriters: Ghostwriters create content for clients or employers, but their work is published under someone else's name. Ghostwriters may write articles, books, or other types of content.

Grant writers: Grant writers create proposals and applications for funding from foundations, government agencies, and other sources. They may write grant proposals, letters of inquiry, and other types of content.

Medical writers: Medical writers create content related to the medical field, such as patient education materials, medical journal articles, and drug information sheets.

Marketing writers: Marketing writers create content that promotes a product or service. They may write press releases, brochures, and other types of marketing materials.

News writers: News writers create content for news websites or publications. They may write articles, interviews, and other types of content that cover current events and breaking news.

SEO writers: SEO writers create content that is optimized for search engines, using targeted keywords and other SEO techniques to increase the visibility of a website or blog.
Guide to Building a Blog Content Strategy
Here is a step-by-step guide to building a blog content strategy:

Identify your audience: The first step in building a content strategy is to identify your target audience. Who are you writing for, and what are their interests and needs?

Define your goals: Next, think about what you want to achieve with your blog. Are you trying to inform, educate, persuade, or entertain your readers? Your goals will help to guide the content you create.

Research your topic: Research potential topics for your blog to get ideas and gather information. Look for gaps in the market and consider what your audience will find most valuable and interesting.

Create a content calendar: A content calendar is a schedule of the content you plan to publish on your blog. It can help you stay organized and ensure that you are consistently publishing new content.

Write high-quality content: Focus on creating high-quality, engaging content that meets the needs and interests of your audience. Use relevant and targeted keywords to optimize your content for search engines.

Promote your content: Promote your blog through social media, email newsletters, and other channels to attract more readers and increase traffic to your site.

Analyze and refine your strategy: Use analytics tools to track the performance of your blog and see what's working and what's not. Use this information to refine your content strategy and make improvements.

Remember, building a successful content strategy takes time and dedication. Be patient and keep working on your strategy, and you will eventually see results.

Website For Content Writing Examples:
Here are a few examples of website content writing:

Homepage: The homepage of a website is typically the first page that visitors see, so it's important to make a good impression. A homepage should clearly state what the website is about and provide a clear call to action for visitors.
Example:

Welcome to our website! We offer a variety of high-quality products for your home and garden. From stylish furniture to unique planters, we have something for every taste and budget. Check out our featured items below, or use the navigation menu to browse our full selection.

Product page: A product page should provide detailed information about a specific product, including its features, benefits, and price. It should also include high-quality images and possibly videos to help visitors visualize the product.
Example:
Introducing the newest addition to our kitchen appliance line: the Smart Blender. With its advanced technology and sleek design, this blender is perfect for smoothie lovers and home chefs alike.

Powerful motor: The Smart Blender has a 1500-watt motor that can handle even the toughest ingredients with ease.
Multiple settings: Choose from smoothie, chop, grind, and puree settings to get perfect consistency every time.
Easy to clean: The blender's detachable parts are dishwasher safe, so clean-up is a breeze.

About us page: An about us page should provide information about a company's history, mission, and values. It should also include information about the team behind the company and any awards or certifications they may have received.

Example:

At XYZ Company, we have been serving the community for over 20 years. Our mission is to provide the highest quality products and services to our customers. We believe in treating every customer with respect and going above and beyond to ensure their satisfaction.

Our team is made up of dedicated professionals with years of experience in their respective fields. We are constantly striving to improve and stay up-to-date on the latest industry trends. In recognition of our commitment to excellence, we have received numerous awards and certifications. We are proud to be a trusted resource for our customers.

Why is it important to improve your content writing skills?

Improving your content writing skills can help you to create more effective and engaging written content, which can in turn help to improve the overall performance and effectiveness of your content. This may include attracting more readers, generating more leads or sales, or building a stronger online presence or brand.

What are some tips for improving your content writing skills?
Some tips for improving your content writing skills include:

Reading and studying the work of other writers, particularly those whose writing style or subject matter you admire
Practicing regularly by writing on a variety of topics and for different audiences
Seeking feedback and criticism from other writers or editors
Taking online courses or workshops to learn new techniques and strategies
Using writing prompts or exercises to help stimulate creativity and improve your writing skills
Keeping up to date with industry trends and best practices in content creation

How do I write clear and concise content?

To write clear and concise content, try the following tips:

Start with a strong, clear headline or topic sentence that captures the main idea of your content

Use subheadings and bullet points to break up the content and improve readability

Avoid using unnecessary words or phrases, and eliminate jargon or technical language that may be confusing to your readers

Use strong, descriptive language and engaging storytelling techniques to convey your message effectively

Edit and proofread your content to ensure it is error-free and polished

How do I make my content more engaging?

To make your content more engaging, consider the following tips:

Use a conversational tone and write as if you are speaking directly to your reader

Use storytelling techniques to bring your content to life and make it more relatable

Use images, videos, and other visual elements to add interest and break up the text
Use strong, descriptive language and engaging adjectives to create a sense of intrigue and curiosity
Provide valuable, informative, and useful content to your readers
Conclude with a call to action or next steps for your readers
How do I improve the readability of my content?
To improve the readability of your content, try the following tips:
Use short, simple sentences and paragraphs
Use headings and subheadings to break up the text and help guide the reader
Use bullet points and numbered lists to highlight key points
Use images and other visual elements to break up the text and add interest
Use appropriate font sizes and styles to improve readability
Avoid using too much bold or italicized text, as this can be distracting to the reader

How do I proofread and edit my content?
To proofread and edit your content, try the following tips:

Use spell check and grammar check tools to catch any errors
Read your content out loud to help catch any mistakes or awkward phrases

How to Improve Your Content Writing in 15 Steps?

Here are 15 steps you can take to improve your content writing:

Set clear goals: Before you start writing, it's important to know what you want to achieve with your content. Do you want to inform, persuade, or entertain your audience? Clearly defining your goals will help you create content that is targeted and effective.

Understand your audience: To create content that resonates with your audience, you need to know who they are and what they are looking for. Consider factors such as their age, location, interests, and pain points.

Research your topic: Gather as much information as you can about your topic. This will help you create content that is accurate and comprehensive.

Use a clear structure: Organize your content in a logical and easy-to-follow way. Use headings, subheadings, and bullet points to break up the text and make it easier to read.

Write an engaging introduction: The first few sentences of your content should grab the reader's attention and set the tone for the rest of the piece.

Use strong headlines: A strong headline is crucial for getting people to read your content. Make sure your headline is clear, concise, and attention-grabbing.

Use simple, straightforward language: Avoid using jargon or technical language that your audience may not understand. Instead, use simple, straightforward language that is easy to read and comprehend.

Use active voice: Writing in the active voice makes your content more engaging and easier to read. Instead of saying "The cake was baked by Mary," say "Mary baked the cake."

Use transition words: Transition words help to link your ideas and make your content flow more smoothly. Examples include "however," "in addition," and "furthermore."

Edit and proofread: Take the time to carefully edit and proofread your content to ensure that it is error-free.

Use images and other media: Including images, videos, and other media can make your content more engaging and visually appealing. Just make sure to use high-quality, relevant media.

Use internal and external links: Linking to other relevant content on your website or to external sources can add value to your content and help to establish your credibility.

Keep it concise: Long blocks of text can be overwhelming and off-putting to readers.

Aim to keep your content concise and to the point.

Vary your sentence length: Varying the length of your sentences can make your writing more interesting and easier to read. Mix up short and long sentences to add variety and rhythm to your content.

Get feedback: Seek feedback from others, such as colleagues or friends, to get a fresh perspective on your writing. This can help you identify areas for improvement and ensure that your content is effective.

What is an Infographic?

An Infographic is a visual representation of information or data that is designed to convey complex information in a simple, easy-to-understand format. Infographics may include text, images, charts, graphs, maps, and other visual elements to help illustrate and explain the information being presented.

Why use infographics in content?
Infographics can be a powerful tool for enhancing the effectiveness and engagement of your content. They can help to break up long blocks of text, make

complex information easier to understand and add visual interest to your content. Info graphics can also be shared on social media and other platforms, which can help to increase the reach and visibility of your content.

How do I use info graphics in my content?
To use info graphics in your content, consider the following tips:

Identify the purpose and goal of your info graphic. What information are you trying to convey and what
Is the best way to present it visually? Gather and organize the data or information that you want to include in your info graphic. This may involve conducting research, collecting statistics, or creating charts and graphs.
Choose a design style and layout that is appropriate for your info graphic. Consider the type and amount of information you are presenting, as well as the overall tone and purpose of your content.
Use a combination of text, images, charts, graphs, and other visual elements to illustrate and explain the information in your infographic.

Use a consistent color scheme and font style to create visual unity and coherence. Keep your info graphic simple and easy to understand. Avoid including too much information or using too many complex visual elements.
Test your info graphic to ensure that it is effective and engaging.

How do I create high-quality info graphics?
To create high-quality info graphics, consider the following tips:
Use accurate and reliable sources for your data and information.
Use clear and concise text that is easy to read and understand.
Use appropriate visual elements to illustrate and explain your data.
Keep your design simple and clean, and use a consistent color scheme and font style.
Test your info graphic to ensure that it is effective and engaging.
Use a tool or service that allows you to easily create and customize your infographic, such as Canva or Piktochart.

To promote your info graphics, consider the following tips:

Share your info graphics on social media platforms and other websites.

Embed your info graphics in relevant blog posts or articles.

Include a link to your info graphic in your email signature or newsletters.

Use relevant hash tags when sharing your info graphic on social media.

Offer to share your info graphic with other bloggers or websites in your industry in exchange for a link back to your website.

How do I measure the success of my infographics?

To measure the success of your info graphics, consider tracking the following metrics:

The number of views or impressions your info graphic receives

The number of shares or social media engagements your info graphic

Info graphics can be a powerful tool for improving the quality and effectiveness of your content. Here are some tips for using info graphics to enhance your content:

Choose a clear and compelling topic: Start by selecting a topic that is relevant and interesting to your audience. The topic should be something that can be easily explained through visual elements.

Gather data and information: Once you have a topic, research and gather data and information that will help you create a clear and accurate info graphic.

Organize the data: Organize the data in a logical and easy-to-understand way. Use headings, subheadings, and bullet points to break up the information and make it easier to read.

Choose a design style: Decide on a design style that is appropriate for your topic and audience. Consider factors such as the tone, color palette, and layout that will best convey your message.

Use clear and concise language: Info graphics should be easy to understand, so use clear and concise language that is easy to read and comprehend. Avoid using jargon or technical language.

Use visual elements effectively: Use visual elements such as charts, graphs, and icons to help illustrate your points and make the information more engaging.

Use a consistent design: Use a consistent design throughout the infographic to create a cohesive and professional look.

Check for accuracy: Before publishing the infographic, double-check the data and information to ensure that it is accurate and up-to-date.

Promote the info graphic: Once you have created the info graphic, promote it through social media, email marketing, and other channels to reach a wider audience.

Measure the success of the info graphic: Use analytics tools to track the success of your info graphic and identify areas for improvement.

Basic Info graphics tools for a content writer:

There are many tools available that can help content writers create high-quality info graphics. Here are a few basic tools that you may find useful:

Canvas: Canvas is a user-friendly design tool that offers a wide range of templates and design elements for creating info graphics and other visual content.

Pikto chart: Pikto chart is a powerful info graphic maker that offers a variety of templates, icons, and charts to help you create professional-looking info graphics.

Venngage: Venngage is another popular info graphic maker that offers a range of templates and design elements for creating engaging info graphics.

Adobe Illustrator: Adobe Illustrator is a powerful design tool that allows you to create detailed and complex info graphics from scratch. It is more advanced than some of the other tools on this list, so it may be more suitable for experienced designers.

Info gram: Info gram is a user-friendly info graphic maker that offers a range of templates, charts, and maps to help you create professional-looking info graphics.

Remember to always use high-quality, relevant images and data when creating info graphics, and be sure to double-check the accuracy of the information before publishing.

What is a writing style?

A writing style is a way that an author or writer chooses to express themselves through their written work. It can refer to the tone, voice, and language that the writer uses, as well as the structure and organization of the content. Different writing styles may be appropriate for different types of writing and audiences.

How do I choose a topic and style of writing?
To choose a topic and style of writing, consider the following tips:

Identify the purpose and goal of your writing. Are you writing to inform, entertain, persuade, or express yourself? This will help to guide your choice of topic and style.
Consider your audience. Who will be reading your writing and what interests or needs do they have? Choose a topic and style that is relevant and engaging to your audience.
Consider your own interests and passions. What topics or themes are you most passionate about or knowledgeable about? Choosing a topic that you are genuinely interested in can help to make the writing process more enjoyable and authentic.
Experiment with different styles and tones. Try writing in different styles and see which one feels most natural and effective for you.
Seek feedback from others. Ask for feedback from friends, colleagues, or

writing mentors to help you identify your strengths and areas for improvement.

Some common writing styles include:
Persuasive: A persuasive writing style is designed to convince the reader to take a particular action or adopt a particular point of view. It often includes strong, emotive language and may use rhetorical devices to make an argument.
Narrative: A narrative writing style tells a story or relates an experience. It often uses descriptive language and may include dialogue or character development.
Descriptive: A descriptive writing style is designed to paint a picture or describe a person, place, or thing in detail. It often uses sensory language and may include figurative language or imagery.
Expository: An expository writing style is designed to explain or inform.

Here are some tips for choosing a topic and style of writing:

Identify your audience: Consider who you are writing for and what their interests and needs are. This will help you choose a topic that is relevant and engaging for your audience.

Consider your goals: Think about what you want to achieve with your writing. Are you trying to inform, educate, persuade, or entertain your readers? This will help you choose a topic and style that is appropriate for your goals.

Research your topic: Once you have identified a potential topic, do some research to see what has already been written about it and to gather ideas and information.

Choose a style that fits your topic: Consider the tone and style that will be most effective for your topic and audience. For example, a humorous or light-hearted style may be appropriate for a casual blog post, while a more formal and authoritative style may be better for a research paper.

Be authentic: Choose a topic and style that reflects your own interests and personality. Being authentic and genuine will help to make your writing more engaging and enjoyable for your readers.

What are common mistakes in writing content?
Here are some common mistakes to avoid when writing content:

Failing to plan and organize your content: It's important to have a clear idea of what you want to say and how you want to say it before you start writing. Take the time to outline your content and gather all necessary information before you begin.

Being too vague or general: Avoid using vague or general language that doesn't convey any specific meaning or value. Instead, be specific and provide concrete examples to illustrate your points.

Failing to proofread and edit: Proofreading and editing are important steps in the writing process. Make sure to carefully review your content for errors in grammar, spelling, punctuation, and style.

Not considering your audience: Consider who your audience is and what they are looking for when writing your content. Tailor your language and style to meet the needs and interests of your readers.

Being too wordy or repetitive: Keep your content concise and to the point. Avoid using unnecessary words or repeating the same information over and over.

Neglecting SEO: If you are writing for the web, make sure to include relevant keywords and optimize your content for search engines. This can help to improve the visibility and reach of your content.

Ignoring readability: Make sure your content is easy to read and understand. Use headings, subheadings, bullet points, and other formatting elements to improve readability and make your content more visually appealing.

Using jargon or technical language: Avoid using jargon or technical language that may be confusing or off-putting to your readers. Instead, use clear, simple language that is easy to understand.

Failing to provide value: Make sure your content provides value to your readers. This may involve sharing useful information, offering helpful tips or advice, or providing unique insights or perspectives.

Neglecting to include a call to action: If you want your readers to take a specific action, make sure to include a clear call to action in your content. This could be as simple as asking them to share your content or signing up for your email list.

How Much Do Content Writers Get Pay?

The pay for content writers can vary widely depending on a number of factors, including their level of experience, the type of content they are writing, and the industry in which they are working. Some content writers may work on a freelance basis and set their own rates, while others may be employed by a company or agency and receive a salary or hourly rate.

According to data from the Bureau of Labor Statistics, the median hourly wage for writers and authors was $24.98 in 2020.

However, this figure includes writers of all types, and content writers may earn less or more depending on their specific job duties and experience. Some content writers may earn an hourly rate of $20 to $30 per hour, while others may earn $50 or more per hour for more specialized or technical content.

It is also important to note that content writers may work on a project basis, in which they are paid a flat fee for a specific piece of content or a series of articles. In these cases, the pay may be higher or lower depending on the length and complexity of the project, as well as the writer's level of expertise.

What are the different types of content writing?

There are many different types of content writing, including

Web copy: Web copy is written content that appears on a website. It may include homepage content, product descriptions, landing pages, and more. Web copy should be concise, clear, and focused on the needs and interests of the target audience.

Blog posts: Blog posts are written articles that are published on a website or blog. They may cover a wide range of topics and may be used to inform, educate, or entertain readers.

Articles: Articles are longer pieces of written content that may be published in a magazine, newspaper, or online. Articles may be informative, educational, or opinion-based.

Social media posts: Social media posts are written updates that are shared on social media platforms. They may include text, images, links, and other media and should be concise, engaging, and tailored to the platform and audience.

Press releases: Press releases are written announcements that are distributed to media outlets. They may announce news, events, or other updates related to a business, organization, or individual.

Marketing materials: Marketing materials are written materials that are used to promote a product, service, or brand. This may include sales letters, brochures, emails, and more.

Some best practices for content writing include:

Identify your audience and purpose: Before you start writing, consider who your audience is and what you want to accomplish with your content. This will help to guide your choice of topic and tone.

Research your topic: Gather all necessary information and sources before

Content writing refers to the creation of written content for the purpose of publishing it online or in print. It includes creating written content for websites, blogs, social media platforms, marketing materials, and other forms of media.

There are several types of content writing, including

SEO writing: This type of writing is focused on optimizing web content for search engines. It involves using keywords and phrases in a way that helps a website rank higher in search results.

Blog writing: This type of writing involves creating content for a blog, which can be about any topic or theme.

Technical writing: This type of writing involves creating content about technical subjects or products, such as software or hardware manuals.

Marketing writing: This type of writing involves creating content for marketing materials, such as brochures, emails, and advertisements.

Ghostwriting: This type of writing involves creating content on behalf of someone else, who is credited as the author.

Creative writing: This type of writing involves creating original content for fiction or nonfiction purposes, such as novels, short stories, or articles.

Academic writing: This type of writing involves creating content for academic purposes, such as research papers or thesis statements.

Content Writing Tips for Beginners

Here are some tips for beginners who are looking to improve their content writing skills:

Start with a clear purpose: Before you start writing, it's important to have a clear understanding of what you want to achieve with your content. This could be to inform, persuade, or entertain your audience.

Use a catchy headline: The headline of your content is often the first thing that readers will see, so it's important to make it compelling and informative.

Keep it simple: Use clear and concise language, and avoid using jargon or technical terms that your audience may not understand.

Use subheadings: Subheadings can help break up your content and make it easier for readers to scan and understand.

Use images and other media: Including images and other media, such as videos or infographics, can help to make your content more engaging and visually appealing.

Use active voice: Using the active voice can make your writing more engaging and easier to understand.

Edit and proofread: Always take the time to edit and proofread your content to ensure that it is error-free and reads well.

Use SEO techniques: If you are writing for the web, it's important to use SEO techniques, such as keyword research and meta descriptions, to help your content rank well in search results.

Write for your audience: Keep your audience in mind as you write, and focus on writing content that will be relevant and valuable to them.

Practice regularly: The more you practice writing, the better you will become.

Consider setting aside time each week to write and hone your skills.

Difference between a content writer and a content creator:

A content writer is someone who is responsible for creating written content for a website or other platform. This can include blog posts, articles, website copy, and other types of written content. Content creation, on the other hand, refers to the process of creating any type of content for a website or other platform. This can include written content, but it can also include other types of content such as images, videos, audio, or other media.

In other words, a content writer is focused specifically on creating written content, while a content creator may create a variety of different types of content. Both roles may involve researching topics, developing ideas, and creating content that is engaging and informative for the intended audience.

Difference between a content writer and a copywriter:

A content writer is someone who is responsible for creating written content for a website or other platform. This can include blog posts, articles, website copy, and other types of written content. The goal of a content writer is usually to inform, educate, or entertain the audience, rather than to sell a product or service.

A copywriter, on the other hand, is a professional writer who creates persuasive marketing materials, such as sales letters, advertisements, and website content. The goal of a copywriter is to sell a product or service by writing persuasive and compelling copy that inspires the reader to take action.

In other words, content writers focus on creating informative and engaging written content, while copywriters focus on creating persuasive marketing materials that are designed to sell a product or service.

How do you write a content writing sample for beginners?
Here are some tips for writing a content writing sample as a beginner:

Choose a topic that you are passionate about or have some knowledge of. This will make it easier for you to write and will also make your writing more authentic and engaging.

Research your topic thoroughly. Gather information from a variety of sources, including online articles, books, and expert opinions. This will help you understand the topic more fully and give you a strong foundation for your writing.

Outline your content. Organize your ideas into an outline to help you stay focused and structured as you write.

Write a catchy headline. Your headline should be attention-grabbing and accurately reflect the content of your article.

Start with an introduction. Use your introduction to introduce your topic and hook your reader's attention.

Use subheadings and bullet points. Subheadings and bullet points help to break up your content and make it easier to read.

Use examples and anecdotes to illustrate your points. This will help your reader understand and relate to your content.

Conclude your article with a strong conclusion. Summarize your main points and leave your reader with something to think about.

Edit and proofread your writing. Check for grammar and spelling errors, and make sure your writing flows logically and is easy to understand.

Seek feedback from others. Ask someone you trust to review your writing and give you constructive feedback. This will help you improve your writing skills and become a better content writer.

The format of content writing can vary depending on the specific requirements of the project or the preferences of the writer. However, there are some general guidelines that can be followed when writing content:

Use a clear and concise writing style: Avoid jargon and unnecessary words, and focus on making your points in a straightforward and easy-to-understand manner.

Use headings and subheadings to break up your content and make it easier to scan: This can help your readers quickly find the information they are looking for.

Use bullet points and numbered lists to highlight key points: This can make your content more visually appealing and easier to read.

Use short paragraphs and sentences to make your content easier to read: This can help keep your readers from getting overwhelmed or losing interest.

Use active voice instead of passive voice: This can make your writing more engaging and easier to understand.

Use transitional phrases to connect your ideas and make your content flow smoothly: This can help your readers follow your line of thinking and make your content more cohesive.

Use quotes and examples to illustrate your points: This can help add credibility and depth to your content.

Use proper grammar, spelling, and punctuation: This can help make your content more professional and polished.

Use SEO best practices to optimize your content for search engines: This can help your content rank higher in search results and drive more traffic to your website.

Link to reputable sources to add credibility and depth to your content: This can help your readers trust your content and find more information on the topic.

Include a call to action to encourage your readers to take a specific action: This can help you achieve your goals for your content and drive engagement.

Use formatting to make your content easier to read and more visually appealing: This can include using bold and italicized text, using bullet points and numbered lists, and using headings and subheadings.

What does a content writer do?

A content writer is responsible for creating written content for various media, including websites, blogs, social media platforms, marketing materials, and more. The specific tasks of a content writer may include:

Researching and identifying topics to write about
Writing and editing content, including blog posts, articles, and marketing materials
Optimizing content for search engines (SEO)
Collaborating with team members, such as designers and marketing professionals

Proofreading and fact-checking content to ensure accuracy
Staying up-to-date with industry trends and best practices
A content writer may work in a variety of industries and sectors, including marketing, advertising, media, and publishing. They may also work as freelancers or be employed by a company. The job may require a combination of writing and editing skills, as well as knowledge of SEO and digital marketing principles.

How to learn content writing with a step-wise procedure?

Content writing is the process of creating written content for websites, blogs, social media, marketing materials, and other platforms. It involves researching, brainstorming, and writing content that is informative, engaging, and valuable to the target audience.

Here are some steps you can follow to learn content writing:

Understand your audience: The first step in content writing is understanding who your target audience is. This will help you tailor your content to their needs and interests.

Research your topic: Before you start writing, it's important to do thorough research on your topic. This will help you understand the subject matter and ensure that your content is accurate and informative.

Brainstorm ideas: Once you have a good understanding of your topic, start brainstorming ideas for your content. Think about what your audience might be interested in and what you can offer them.

Create an outline: Once you have a list of ideas, create an outline to organize your thoughts and structure your content. This will help you stay focused and make the writing process easier.

Write your content: Now it's time to start writing your content. Use clear, concise language and follow best practices for grammar and style.

Edit and proofread: Before you publish your content, make sure to edit and proofread it to ensure that it is error-free and easy to read.

Publish and promote: Once your content is complete, publish it on your website or platform of choice and promote it to your target audience.

By following these steps and practicing regularly, you can improve your content writing skills over time.

How to write plagiarism-free content writing in 10 steps?

Understand what plagiarism is: Plagiarism is the act of copying or using someone else's work or ideas without proper attribution. It is important to understand what plagiarism is and to avoid it in your own writing.

Use your own words: To avoid plagiarism, it is important to use your own words and ideas when writing. Avoid copying and pasting text from other sources or heavily paraphrasing without giving credit.

Cite your sources: Whenever you use information or ideas from another source, make sure to properly cite the source. This can be done using in-text citations or a bibliography at the end of your document.

Use quotation marks: If you do need to include text directly from another source, use quotation marks to indicate that the words are not your own. Make sure to also include an in-text citation or reference to the original source.

Use a plagiarism checker: There are several online tools that can help you to check your writing for plagiarism. These tools can scan your text and highlight any potential instances of plagiarism, allowing you to make the necessary changes before publishing your work.

Understand copyright laws: Be aware of copyright laws and the rights of the original authors or creators of the content you are using. Make sure to obtain permission before using any copyrighted material in your own writing.

Be careful when using online content: Be wary of using content from the internet in your own writing, as it may be copyrighted or protected by intellectual property laws.

Instead, try to find reputable sources and always give credit where credit is due.

Keep good records: Keep track of the sources you use and make sure to properly cite them in your writing. This will help you to avoid accidental plagiarism and ensure that you are giving credit where it is due.

Understand paraphrasing: Paraphrasing is the act of rephrasing someone else's ideas or words in your own words. While paraphrasing can be a useful way to incorporate information from other sources into your own writing, it is important to make sure that you are not simply copying and pasting the text and to properly cite the original source.

Seek help if needed: If you are unsure about how to properly use and cite sources in your writing, seek help from a tutor, writing center, or other resources. It is better to ask for help and get it right than to risk committing plagiarism.

There are many different plagiarism checker tools available online, both free and paid. Here are a few options to consider:

Turnitin: Turn tin is a popular plagiarism checker tool that is commonly used by schools and universities. It can scan a wide range of documents and highlight potential instances of plagiarism.

Plag Scan: Plag Scan is a cloud-based plagiarism detection tool that can scan documents of up to 50,000 words. It offers a range of features, including a bulk check option and the ability to exclude certain sources from the scan.

Copyleaks: Copyleaks is a plagiarism checker that uses artificial intelligence to scan documents for potential instances of plagiarism. It can scan documents in multiple languages and offers a range of customization options.

PlagiarismCheckerX: PlagiarismCheckerX is a plagiarism detection tool that can scan a wide range of file types, including PDFs and Word documents. It also offers a range of features, including the ability to compare multiple documents at once and a built-in text editor.

Grammarly: Grammarly is a writing tool that can check for grammar and spelling errors, as well as potential instances of plagiarism. It offers a range of features, including a plagiarism checker and a thesaurus.

Plagiarisma: Plagiarisma is a free plagiarism checker that can scan documents in over 190 languages. It offers a range of features, including the ability to exclude certain sources from the scan and the option to receive a report on the originality of your document.

Duplichecker: Duplichecker is a free plagiarism checker that can scan documents of up to 10,000 words. It offers a range of features, including the ability to exclude certain sources from the scan and the option to receive a report on the originality of your document.

Quetext: Quetext is a plagiarism checker that uses artificial intelligence to scan documents for potential instances of plagiarism. It offers a range of features, including the ability to scan documents in multiple languages and the option to customize the sensitivity of the scan.

How to Start Content Writing On Quora and Social Media?

Starting content writing on Quora and social media can be a great way to practice your writing skills, share your knowledge and expertise with a wider audience, and potentially even earn money through sponsored content. Here are some steps you can follow to get started:

Set up your profile: To start writing on Quora or social media, you'll need to create a profile. Make sure to include a clear profile picture and bio that accurately represents who you are and what you do.

Choose your topics: On Quora, you can answer questions on a variety of topics, so take some time to think about the areas you are most knowledgeable and passionate about. On social media, you can create your own content or share content related to your interests and expertise.

Research your topic: Before you start writing, it's important to do thorough research on your topic to ensure that your content is accurate and informative. This will also help you come up with fresh ideas and perspectives.

Write your content: Once you have a good understanding of your topic, start writing your content. Use clear, concise language and follow best practices for grammar and style.

Edit and proofread: Before you publish your content, make sure to edit and proofread it to ensure that it is error-free and easy to read.

Publish and promote: Once your content is complete, publish it on Quora or your chosen social media platform and promote it to your target audience. This can help you reach a wider audience and potentially even earn money through sponsored content.

By following these steps and practicing regularly, you can become a successful content writer on Quora and social media.

Starting a content writing freelance career can be a great way to earn a living while doing something you love. Here are some steps you can take to get started:

Develop your writing skills: In order to succeed as a content writer, you'll need to have strong writing skills. This includes being able to write clearly and concisely, as well as having good grammar and spelling skills. Consider taking a writing course or workshop to improve your skills.

Choose your niche: Think about what topics you enjoy writing about and what you have expertise in. This will help you to focus your efforts and make it easier to find work.

Build your portfolio: To show potential clients what you're capable of, you'll need to have a portfolio of your work. Start by writing a few samples in your chosen niche and then compile them into a document or website that you can share with potential clients.

Find clients: There are many ways to find clients as a freelance content writer. Some options include networking, pitching to businesses and websites directly, or joining freelance job boards or online marketplaces.

Set your rates and terms: Decide how much you want to charge for your services and what terms you're willing to work under. Be sure to research what other writers in your niche are charging so you can set competitive rates.

Promote yourself: To get your name out there, consider creating a website or blog to showcase your work, joining writing communities or forums, and building a social media presence. This will help you to attract more clients and build your reputation as a content writer.

30 Content Writing Examples and How To Tips for Website Articles?

Here are 30 content writing examples and tips for writing website articles:

How to start a garden from scratch
The benefits of meditation for stress reduction
10 easy ways to reduce plastic waste
How to create a budget and stick to it
The top 10 best hiking trails in the U.S.
The benefits of a plant-based diet
How to create a successful online business
The history of chocolate and its health benefits
How to design a website using WordPress
The top 10 best beaches in the world
How to create a social media marketing strategy
The benefits of learning a second language
How to create a budget-friendly home gym
The top 10 best movies of all time
How to create a successful email marketing campaign
The benefits of practicing yoga
How to create a successful Kickstarter campaign
The top 10 best books of all time

How to create a successful e-commerce website?
The benefits of learning how to code
How to create a successful podcast

The top 10 best travel destinations in the world
How to create a successful online course
The benefits of meditation for productivity
How to create a successful YouTube channel
The top 10 best restaurants in the world
How to create a successful affiliate marketing program
The benefits of learning a musical instrument
How to create a successful mobile app
The top 10 best music festivals in the world
Tips for writing website articles:

Choose a topic that is interesting and relevant to your audience.
Research your topic thoroughly and gather information from a variety of sources.
Organize your ideas into an outline to help you stay focused and structured as you write.
Use subheadings and bullet points to break up your content and make it easier to read.
Use examples and anecdotes to illustrate your points and make your content more engaging.
Edit and proofread your writing to ensure accuracy and clarity.

Use appropriate keywords to optimize your content for search engines.
Include internal and external links to further support your content and provide additional resources for your readers.

The Importance of Strong Titles in Content Marketing:

The title of your content is often the first thing that a reader sees, and it plays a crucial role in whether or not they decide to click and read more. A strong title not only captures the attention of your audience but also gives them an idea of what they can expect to read in the article.

In the world of content marketing, a compelling title can make all the difference in driving traffic and engagement.

In addition to being attention-grabbing, a good title should also be clear and concise, accurately reflecting the topic of your article. This is especially important for search engine optimization (SEO), as the title is one of the first things that search engines consider when ranking content. By including relevant keywords and phrases in your title, you can improve the chances of your content being discovered by the right audience.

Overall, the importance of strong titles in content marketing cannot be overstated. Whether you are writing a blog post, an article, or any other type of online content, crafting a compelling title is essential for attracting and retaining readers.

Clearly and Concisely Communicate the Topic of Your Article

When it comes to writing effective titles, it's important to clearly and concisely communicate the topic of your article. A title that is too vague or misleading can turn off readers, leading them to click away before they even start reading. On the other hand, a title that accurately reflects the content of your article can help draw in the right audience and keep them engaged.

One way to ensure that your title clearly communicates the topic of your article is to be as specific as possible. Instead of using general terms or broad subjects, try to get to the heart of what your article is about by using a more specific language. For example, "5 Tips for Planning the Perfect Vacation" is more specific and informative than "Vacation Planning 101."

In addition to being specific, it's also important to keep your title concise. While you want to be clear about the topic of your article, you don't want to use too many words or make your title too long. Aim for a title that is easy to read and quickly gets to the point.

By clearly and concisely communicating the topic of your article in your title, you can help attract the right audience and keep them engaged. This is essential for building trust and credibility with your readers, as well as improving the chances of your content being shared and discovered by a wider audience.

How to Create compelling content with better words?
Here are some tips for creating compelling content with better words:

Choose the right words for your audience. Use language that is appropriate for your audience's level of understanding and interests.

Use active voice instead of passive voice. Active voice makes your writing more direct and engaging, whereas passive voice can make it sound dull and disconnected.

Use strong verbs. Strong verbs convey action and add emphasis to your writing. For example, "run" is a stronger verb than "walk."

Use descriptive language. Descriptive language helps paint a vivid picture in the reader's mind and makes your content more engaging.

Avoid jargon and technical terms. Unless your audience is familiar with these terms, they can be confusing and detract from your message.

Use concrete language instead of abstract language. Concrete language is specific and sensory, whereas abstract language is general and vague.

Avoid using cliches. Cliches are overused and can make your content sound unoriginal and uninspired.

Vary your sentence structure. Mixing up your sentence structure can make your writing more interesting and engaging.

Use transitional words and phrases to connect your ideas. Transitional words and phrases help to create a logical flow in your writing.

Use powerful words. Power words are words that elicit an emotional response and can help to make your content more compelling. Examples include "amazing," "incredible," and "unforgettable."

By following these tips, you can create compelling content that resonates with

your audience and effectively communicates your message.

How to Use Topic Tools for Inspiring Content writers?

There are several topic tools that can be used to help inspire content writers, including

Google's Keyword Planner: This tool allows you to enter a keyword or phrase and see how often it is searched for on Google. You can use this information to identify popular topics and generate ideas for content.

Answer the Public: This tool generates a list of questions related to a given keyword or phrase, which can be used as inspiration for content.

Ahrefs' Content Explorer: This tool allows you to search for articles and blog posts based on a keyword or phrase. You can use this tool to see what topics are currently popular and generate ideas for your own content.

SEMrush's Topic Research: This tool allows you to enter a keyword or phrase and generates a list of related topics, as well as information on the level of demand and competition for each topic.

Buzzsumo: This tool allows you to enter a keyword or phrase and see the most shared content on social media for that topic. You can use this information to identify popular topics and generate ideas for your own content.

By using these tools, you can generate a list of potential topics for your content and use them as inspiration for your writing. It's important to remember to tailor your content to your audience and ensure that it is relevant, valuable, and engaging.

Here are some steps you can take to train yourself to be a content writer:

Build your writing skills: To become a successful content writer, you will need strong writing skills. Consider taking a course or workshop to improve your writing techniques and learn about different writing styles.

Read widely: Reading is a great way to improve your writing skills and expand your knowledge. Read a variety of material, including articles, blog posts, and books, to expose yourself to different writing styles and techniques.

Practice, practice, practice: The best way to improve your writing skills is to write regularly. Start a personal blog or write for online publications to get experience and build your portfolio.

Learn about SEO: Search engine optimization (SEO) is an important aspect of content writing. Learn about how to use keywords and other SEO techniques to optimize your content for search engines.

Learn about your audience: To create content that resonates with your audience, it's important to understand their needs and interests. Research your target audience and get to know their preferences and behaviors.

Stay up to date: The world of content writing is constantly evolving. Stay up to date on the latest trends and techniques by subscribing to industry blogs and attending conferences or workshops.

Remember, becoming a successful content writer takes time and dedication. Be patient and keep working on your skills, and you will eventually see improvement.

What are the basic skills for a content writer?
The basic skills that are important for content writers to have include:

Strong writing skills: Content writers need to have excellent writing skills in order to create high-quality, engaging content. This includes being able to write clearly and concisely, as well as being able to adapt to different writing styles and tones.

Research skills: Content writers often need to do extensive research in order to write accurate and informative content. They should be able to find and evaluate sources, take notes, and organize information effectively.

Attention to detail: Content writers need to be detail-oriented in order to ensure that their content is error-free and meets the needs of their clients or employers.

Time management skills: Content writers often work on tight deadlines, so it's important for them to be able to manage their time effectively in order to meet their goals.

Collaboration skills: Many content writers work in teams or with clients, so it's important for them to be able to collaborate effectively and communicate their ideas and feedback clearly.

Adaptability: Content writers need to be able to adapt to different writing styles and tones, as well as be able to write about a wide range of topics.

Creativity: Content writers should be able to come up with creative ideas and approaches to writing in order to create engaging and interesting content.

What is difficult in content writing?

Content writing can be as difficult or as easy as you make it. Some people may find it relatively easy to write engaging and informative content, while others may struggle with it. There are a few key factors that can make content writing more or less difficult:

Your writing skills: If you have strong writing skills and are able to write clearly and concisely, content writing may be easier for you. If you struggle with writing or are not confident in your skills, it may be more difficult.

The topic: Some topics may be easier to write about than others, depending on your level of expertise and interest in the subject.

The deadline: Working under tight deadlines can be challenging, especially if you are struggling to come up with ideas or are having difficulty writing.

The purpose of the content: Different types of content (such as educational articles, product descriptions, or promotional materials) may have different goals and requirements, which can affect the difficulty of writing them.

Overall, the difficulty of content writing will depend on your specific circumstances and abilities. With practice and dedication, however, you can improve your skills and become a more confident and effective content writer.

How to start content writing on Fiverr?

To start offering content writing services on Fiverr, follow these steps:

Create an account: Go to the Fiverr website and create an account. You'll need to provide your email address and create a password.

Set up your profile: Once you've created an account, you'll need to set up your profile. This includes adding a profile picture, writing a brief bio, and listing any relevant skills or experience you have.

Create your gig: A gig on Fiverr is a specific service you offer to clients. To create your gig, click on the "Sell" button at the top of the page and follow the prompts. You'll need to choose a category, add a title and description for your gig, and set your rates. You can also add any additional details or requirements you have.

Publish your gig: Once you've created your gig, you'll need to publish it in order for it to be visible to potential clients. To do this, click the "Publish" button at the bottom of the page.

Promote your gig: To increase the visibility of your gig, consider sharing it on social media or promoting it to your network. You can also use Fiverr's promotional tools to increase the chances that your gig will be seen by potential clients.

Remember, to be successful on Fiverr, it's important to deliver high-quality work and maintain good communication with your clients. This will help you to build a positive reputation and attract more business.

What is Content marketing?

Content marketing is a strategic approach to creating and distributing valuable, relevant, and consistent content to attract and retain a clearly defined audience. The goal of content marketing is to drive profitable customer action by building trust and establishing expertise in the eyes of the consumer.

Content marketing involves creating and sharing various types of content, such as blog posts, articles, videos, and social media posts, with the intention of attracting and retaining customers. It is an effective way to engage with potential customers, build relationships, and generate leads.

Content marketing can be used to promote a variety of products and services, and it can be an effective way to reach and engage with a target audience. It can also be used to establish a brand as an authority in its industry and to drive traffic to a website or social media page.

Content marketing is an ongoing process that requires planning, execution, and measurement. It involves creating a content marketing strategy, identifying the target audience, creating content, and promoting and distributing the content to reach the target audience. It also involves analyzing the results of the content marketing efforts to determine what is working and what can be improved.

Overall, content marketing is an effective way to attract and retain customers by providing valuable and relevant content that meets their needs and interests.

What are the benefits of content marketing?
Content marketing can offer a range of benefits, including

Increased brand awareness: By consistently creating and sharing valuable content, you can increase the visibility and awareness of your brand.

Increased website traffic: Well-written and informative content can attract more visitors to your website, which can lead to increased traffic and more opportunities to convert visitors into customers.

Increased lead generation: By offering valuable content in exchange for contact information, you can generate leads and nurture them into customers.

Improved customer engagement: By creating content that addresses the needs and interests of your target audience, you can improve customer engagement and build stronger relationships with your customers.

Better search engine rankings: By creating high-quality, relevant content, you can improve your search engine rankings and make it easier for potential customers to find your website.

There are many different types of content that can be used for content marketing, including

Blog posts: Blog posts are written articles that can be published on a website or blog. They can cover a wide range of topics and can be used to inform, educate, or entertain readers.

Videos: Videos can be a highly effective form of content marketing, as they are easy to share and can be more engaging and interactive than text-based content.

Infographics: Infographics are visual representations of information that can be used to explain complex topics in a more easily digestible format.

Podcasts: Podcasts are audio recordings that can be downloaded and listened to on a variety of devices. They can be a great way to reach a mobile audience and can be used to cover a wide range of topics.

Ebooks: Ebooks are digital books that can be downloaded and read on a variety of devices. They can be a great way to provide in-depth information on a particular topic.

How do I create a content marketing strategy?
To create a content marketing strategy, follow these steps:
Identify your target audience: Determine who your ideal customer is and what their needs and interests are. This will help you to create content that is relevant and valuable to them.

Set your goals: Determine what you want to achieve with your content marketing efforts. This could include increasing brand awareness, generating leads, or driving sales.

Develop a content calendar: Create a plan for when and how often you will publish content. This can help you

20 content writing tips for beginners steps by steps:
Here are 20 steps for beginners to follow to improve their content writing skills:

Start with a clear purpose: Before you start writing, it's important to have a clear understanding of what you want to achieve with your content. This could be to inform, persuade, or entertain your audience.

Choose a topic: Choose a topic that is relevant and interesting to your audience. Conduct research to gather information and ideas for your content.

Create an outline: Organize your ideas and create an outline to help guide your writing process.

Write a catchy headline: The headline of your content is often the first thing that readers will see, so it's important to make it compelling and informative.

Use subheadings: Subheadings can help break up your content and make it easier for readers to scan and understand.

Use active voice: Using the active voice can make your writing more engaging and easier to understand.

Use simple language: Avoid using jargon or technical terms that your audience may not understand. Keep your language clear and concise.

Use examples and anecdotes: Including examples and anecdotes can help to make your content more relatable and engaging.

Use images and other media: Including images and other media, such as videos or infographics, can help to make your content more engaging and visually appealing.

Use transitional phrases: Transitional phrases can help to connect your ideas and make your content flow more smoothly.

Use quotes: Including quotes from experts or other sources can add credibility to your content.

Use lists: Using lists, such as bullet points or numbered lists, can help to make your content easier to read and understand.

Use links: Including links to relevant sources can add value to your content and help to establish credibility.

Use SEO techniques: If you are writing for the web, it's important to use SEO techniques, such as keyword research and meta descriptions, to help your content rank well in search results.

Write for your audience: Keep your audience in mind as you write, and focus on writing content that will be relevant and valuable to them.

Use simple sentence structures: Avoid using complex sentence structures that can be difficult for readers to understand.

Use simple paragraphs: Keep your paragraphs short and to the point to make your content easier to read and understand.

Edit and proofread: Always take the time to edit and proofread your content to ensure that it is error-free and reads well.

Get feedback: Consider seeking feedback from others, such as peers or mentors, to help improve your content writing skills.

Practice regularly: The more you practice writing, the better you will become. Consider setting aside time each week to write and hone your skills.

25 web content writing tips for beginners:

Start with a clear goal in mind: What do you want your readers to do after they read your content? This will help you focus your writing and ensure that your content is clear and effective.

Keep your audience in mind: Consider who you are writing for and tailor your content to their needs, interests, and level of understanding.

Use a clear and concise writing style: Avoid jargon and unnecessary words, and focus on making your points in a straightforward and easy-to-understand manner.

Use headings and subheadings to break up your content and make it easier to scan: This can help your readers quickly find the information they are looking for.

Use bullet points and numbered lists to highlight key points: This can make your content more visually appealing and easier to read.

Use images and videos to break up the text and add visual interest: This can help keep your readers engaged and make your content more memorable.

Use short paragraphs and sentences to make your content easier to read: This can help keep your readers from getting overwhelmed or losing interest.

Use active voice instead of passive voice: This can make your writing more engaging and easier to understand.

Use transitional phrases to connect your ideas and make your content flow smoothly: This can help your readers follow your line of thinking and make your content more cohesive.

Use quotes and examples to illustrate your points: This can help add credibility and depth to your content.

Use proper grammar, spelling, and punctuation: This can help make your content more professional and polished.

Use SEO best practices to optimize your content for search engines: This can help your content rank higher in search results and drive more traffic to your website.

Link to reputable sources to add credibility and depth to your content: This can help your readers trust your content and find more information on the topic.

Include a call to action to encourage your readers to take a specific action: This can help you achieve your goals for your content and drive engagement.

Edit and proofread your content carefully: This can help ensure that your content is error-free and easy to read.

Use a tool like Hemingway to check the readability of your content: This can help you make sure your content is easy to understand for your target audience.

Use a thesaurus to find synonyms and add variety to your vocabulary: This can help you avoid repeating the same words and make your content more engaging.

Use a tool like Grammarly to check your grammar and spelling: This can help you catch errors and improve the overall quality of your content.

Consider hiring a professional editor or proofreader to review your content: This can help you ensure that your content is of the highest quality.

Write in a conversational tone: This can help make your content more relatable and engaging.

Use anecdotes and storytelling to bring your content to life: This can help make your content more memorable and engaging.

Use power words to add emotion and emphasis to your content: This can help make your content more persuasive and impactful.

Use data and statistics to support your arguments: This can help add credibility and depth to your content.

Use formatting to make your content easier to read and more visually appealing: This can include using bold and italicized text, using bullet points and numbered lists, and using headings and subheadings.

Use white space to break up your content.

How can I learn content writing from quora?
There are several ways you can learn content writing from Quora:

Read other content writers' answers: Quora is a great platform for finding high-quality content written by experts in various fields. By reading the answers of successful content writers, you can get an idea of what good content looks like and learn from their writing styles and techniques.

Participate in relevant discussions: Engaging in discussions related to content writing on Quora can help you learn from other's experiences and perspectives. You can also ask questions and seek advice from more experienced content writers.

Follow content writing-related topics: You can follow topics related to content writing on Quora to stay updated on the latest trends and best practices in the industry.

Join content writing communities: There are several content writing communities on Quora where you can connect with

other content writers and learn from their experiences.

Take online courses: Quora also has a number of online courses on content writing that you can take to learn the basics and improve your skills.

In addition to these options, you can also consider reading books and articles about content writing, attending workshops or conferences, and seeking guidance from mentors or professional content-writing services.

Why do some content writers perform better than others?
There are several reasons why some content writers may perform better than others:

Writing skills: Some content writers may have stronger writing skills, including grammar, vocabulary, and clarity of expression, which can make their content more engaging and effective.

Research skills: Good content writers are able to do thorough research and gather reliable and relevant information, which can make their content more informative and credible.

Knowledge of their audience: Successful content writers understand their audience and tailor their content to meet their needs and interests.

SEO knowledge: Content writers who are knowledgeable about SEO best practices are able to optimize their content for search engines, which can help increase its visibility and drive more traffic to their website or blog.

Marketing skills: Content writers who have marketing skills are able to use their content to effectively promote their products or services and drive conversions.

Time management skills: Effective content writers are able to manage their time effectively and meet deadlines consistently, which can help them produce a higher volume of quality content.

Adaptability: Content writers who are able to adapt to changing trends and requirements in the industry are likely to perform better in the long run.

Persistence: Successful content writers are often persistent and willing to put in the time and effort needed to improve their skills and produce high-quality content.

Passion: Content writers who are passionate about their work are likely to be more motivated and produce better results.

Content writing samples:

I can provide you with some tips on how to find content writing samples:

Search online: There are many websites and blogs that publish content writing samples, such as online writing portfolios, writing forums, and content marketing agencies. You can search for keywords like "content writing samples" or "content writing examples" to find a variety of samples.

Look for writing prompts: Many websites and blogs offer writing prompts or challenges to help writers practice their skills and develop new ideas. You can find a variety of content writing samples by searching for writing prompts related to your interests or industry.

Follow content writers on social media: Many content writers share their work on social media platforms like Twitter, LinkedIn, and Instagram. By following content writers you admire, you can find inspiration and see examples of their work. Join writing communities: There are many online writing communities where writers share their work and offer feedback to one another. Joining these communities can be a great way to find content writing samples and connect with other writers.
Take online courses or attend workshops: Many online courses and workshops include writing exercises and prompts that can be used as content writing samples. Taking a course or attending a workshop can also help you learn new skills and improve your writing.

How to write a FAQ about content writing?

What is a content writer?

A content writer is a professional writer who creates written content for websites, blogs, social media, and other online platforms. Content writers research and write articles, blog posts, product descriptions, and other types of written content that are intended to inform, educate, or engage an audience.

What does a content writer do?

A content writer's main responsibility is to create written content that meets the needs and goals of their clients or

employers. This may include researching topics, writing and editing articles, proofreading content, and optimizing content for search engines. Content writers may also be responsible for managing content calendars and creating a content strategy.

How to SEO-optimize in content for search engines?

Here are some tips for SEO-optimizing your content for search engines:

Use relevant and targeted keywords: Research and identify the keywords that your target audience is using to search for information related to your topic. Use these keywords throughout your content, but be sure to use them naturally and avoid keyword stuffing.

Use header tags: Header tags (H1, H2, H3, etc.) help to break up your content and make it easier for readers to scan and understand. They also help search engines understand the hierarchy of your content and give your page a higher ranking.

Use internal and external links: Links to other pages on your website (internal links) and to other reputable websites (external links) can help to improve the credibility and authority of your content.

Use alt tags for images: Alt tags are descriptions that are added to images to help search engines understand what the image is about. Be sure to use descriptive and relevant alt tags for all of the images on your website.

Optimize your title and meta tags: The title and meta tags of your page are important for SEO. The title should be descriptive and include your target keywords, and the meta description should be a short summary of your content that includes your target keywords.

Make your content easy to read: Use short paragraphs, subheadings, and bullet points to make your content easy to read and scan. This can also help to improve the user experience and increase the likelihood that your content will be shared on social media.

How do I become a content writer?
To become a content writer, you will need strong writing skills and the ability to research and organize information. Consider taking a writing course or workshop to improve your skills and gain a better understanding of different writing styles. You may also want to create a portfolio of your writing samples to showcase your skills to potential clients.

How much do content writers get paid?
The pay for content writers can vary widely depending on their level of experience, the type of content they are writing, and the industry in which they are working. Some content writers may work on a freelance basis and set their own rates, while others may be employed by a company or agency

and receive a salary or hourly rate. According to data from the Bureau of Labor Statistics, the median hourly wage for writers and authors was $24.98 in 2020.

What is the difference between a content writer and a copywriter?

Content writing and copywriting are often used interchangeably, but they are slightly different disciplines. Content writing focuses on creating written content for online platforms, such as websites and blogs, with the goal of informing or engaging an audience. Copywriting, on the other hand, involves writing persuasive text with the goal of selling a product or service. Copywriters may create marketing materials such as ads, sales letters, and email campaigns.

Copyright-free content writer template: A content writer template is a document that outlines the structure and content for a specific type of writing, such as an article, blog post, or report. There are many websites that offer free templates for content writing that are licensed for use without the need for attribution or payment. Some options include

Canva: This website offers a wide variety of free templates for content writing, including templates for blog posts, articles, and reports. You can search for templates by keyword or browse through the categories to find the template that best fits your needs.

Hubspot: This website offers a selection of free templates for content writing, including templates for blog posts, articles, and social media posts. You can filter the templates by type and industry to find the template that best fits your needs.

Google Docs: This word-processing software has a variety of templates available for use, including templates for articles, reports, and blog posts. To access the templates, go to "File > New" and select "From template."

Microsoft Word: This word processing software also has a variety of templates available for use, including templates for articles, reports, and blog posts. To access the templates, go to "File > New" and select "From template."

It's important to note that while these templates are free to use, some may have certain licensing terms that you need to adhere to. Be sure to read the terms of use carefully before using any template.

"The Art of Content Writing":

"Defining Your Audience"

"Conducting Effective Research"

"Developing a Unique Voice"

"Crafting Compelling Headlines"

"Structuring Your Content for Maximum Impact"

"Using Images and Other Visual Elements Effectively"

"The Power of Storytelling in Content Writing"

"Using Data and Statistics to Enhance Your Writing"

"SEO Best Practices for Content Writers"

"Creating Engaging Social Media Posts"

"Writing for Email Marketing"

"Crafting Compelling Product Descriptions"

"Writing Effective Landing Pages"

"The Role of Editing in the Writing Process"

"Developing a Content Marketing Strategy"

"Measuring the Success of Your Content"

"Repurposing Your Content for Multiple Channels"

"Collaborating with Other Writers and Editors"

"Writing for International Audiences"

"The Ethics of Content Writing"

"Navigating Legal Issues in Content Writing"

"Writing for Niche Markets"

"The Future of Content Writing"

"Mastering Different Writing Styles"

"Adapting Your Writing for Different Formats"

"Overcoming Writer's Block"

"The Business of Freelance Writing"

"Managing Your Online Presence as a Writer"

"Networking and Building Your Professional Network"

"Continuing Your Education as a Writer"

Defining Your Audience
Chapter: Defining Your Audience

As a content writer, one of the most important things you can do is define your target audience. Your audience is the group of people you are writing for, and understanding who they are and what they need is crucial to creating effective and engaging content. Here are a few tips for defining your audience:

Identify the purpose of your content: Before you can define your audience, you need to know what you are trying to achieve with your writing. Is your goal to inform, educate, entertain, or persuade? This will help you determine the type of audience you are targeting.

Determine the demographics of your audience: Who are the people you are writing for? Are they male or female? What is their age range? What is their level of education? Understanding the demographics of your audience will help you tailor your writing to their specific needs and interests.

Consider their interests and needs: What are your audience's interests and needs?

What problems or challenges are they facing that your content could help solve? Understanding what your audience cares about and what they need will help you create more relevant and useful content.

Think about their level of knowledge: Are you writing for beginners or experts in a particular subject? Understanding your audience's level of knowledge will help you determine the level of detail and complexity to include in your writing.

Defining your audience is an ongoing process, and as you continue to write and publish content, you will likely gain a better understanding of who your readers are and what they are looking for. By keeping your audience in mind as you write, you can create content that resonates with them and meets their needs.

Conducting Effective Research:
As a content writer, conducting effective research is crucial to creating accurate, informative, and engaging content. Research helps you to gather information, verify facts, and understand the context in which you are writing. Here are a few tips for conducting effective research:

Determine your research goals: Before you start researching, it is important to have a clear idea of what you are trying to learn or achieve. This will help you focus your efforts and ensure that you are gathering relevant information.

Identify reliable sources: Not all sources of information are created equal. It is important to use reputable sources that are reliable and accurate. This may include academic journals, government websites, and established news organizations.

Take detailed notes: As you conduct your research, be sure to take detailed notes so that you can easily reference and organize the information you have gathered. It is also a good idea to keep track of your sources so that you can properly cite them in your writing.

Be thorough: It is important to be thorough in your research so that you have a complete understanding of the topic you are writing about. This may require you to consult multiple sources and dig deeper to find relevant information.

Keep an open mind: It is important to approach your research with an open mind and be willing to consider multiple perspectives. This will help you to create a well-rounded and unbiased piece of content.

Effective research is an essential component of successful content writing. By following these tips, you can ensure that your writing is informed, accurate, and engaging.

Developing a Unique Voice
One of the keys to effective content writing is developing a unique voice. Your voice is the way you express yourself through your writing and it can help to set you apart from other writers in your field. Here are a few tips for developing a unique voice:

Know your audience: Understanding your audience will help you determine the tone and style of your writing. For example, if you are writing for a younger audience, you may want to use a more casual and conversational tone.

Find your passion: Write about topics that you are passionate about. This will help you to bring energy and enthusiasm to your writing and make it more engaging for your readers.

Be yourself: Don't try to be someone you're not. Your unique perspective and personality are what make your writing stand out. Be genuine and authentic in your writing and let your voice shine through.

Experiment with different styles: Don't be afraid to try out different writing styles and see what works best for you. This may involve playing with different tones, formats, or lengths of content.

Edit and revise: As you write, be sure to edit and revise your work to ensure that your voice is consistent and clear. This may involve cutting unnecessary words or phrases, rephrasing awkward sentences, and adjusting the tone of your writing.

Developing a unique voice takes time and practice, but it is an essential component of successful content writing. By following these tips, you can begin to find and cultivate your own voice as a writer.

Crafting Compelling Headlines

Headlines are an important element of content writing as they are often the first thing that readers see and can play a big role in whether or not they choose to read on. A compelling headline can grab a reader's attention, pique their curiosity, and encourage them to click through to your content. Here are a few tips for crafting compelling headlines:

Keep it short and sweet: Headlines should be concise and to the point. Aim for around 6-8 words and avoid using unnecessary words or jargon.

Use strong action verbs: Choose verbs that are powerful and active to make your headline more dynamic and engaging.

Include keywords: Incorporating relevant keywords into your headline can help to improve your search engine optimization (SEO) and make your content more discoverable.

Make a promise: Your headline should give readers a sense of what they can expect to get out of your content. Make a promise to your readers and entice them to click through.

Test different versions: Don't be afraid to experiment with different headlines and see which ones perform the best. You can use tools like Google Analytics to track the success of your headlines and see which ones are most effective.

Crafting compelling headlines is an important skill for content writers as it can help to attract and engage readers. By following these tips, you can create headlines that grab attention and encourage readers to click through to your content.

Structuring Your Content for Maximum Impact

The structure of your content plays a crucial role in its effectiveness. A well-structured piece of content is easier to read, understand, and remember, making it more impactful for your audience. Here are a few tips for structuring your content for maximum impact:

Start with an outline: An outline is a helpful tool for organizing your ideas and structuring your content. It can help you to see the big picture and ensure that your content flows logically from one point to the next.

Use headings and subheadings: Headings and subheadings help to break up your content and make it easier to scan and read. They also help to guide your readers through your content and give them a sense of what to expect.

Use lists and bullet points: Lists and bullet points are a great way to present information in a clear and concise manner. They make your content easier to scan and understand, and can help to emphasize key points.

Include transitional phrases: Transitional phrases help to connect your ideas and make your content flow smoothly. They can also help to guide your readers from one point to the next.

Edit and revise: As you structure your content, be sure to edit and revise to ensure that it is clear, concise, and easy to follow. This may involve reordering or combining ideas, or cutting unnecessary information.

Structuring your content effectively is an important aspect of successful writing. By following these tips, you can create content that is easy to read and understand, and that has maximum impact on your audience.

Using Images and Other Visual Elements Effectively

Incorporating visual elements into your content can make it more engaging and memorable for your audience. However, it is important to use these elements effectively in order to maximize their impact. Here are a few tips for using images and other visual elements effectively:

Use high-quality images: Choose images that are clear, well-composed, and relevant to your content. Avoid using low-quality or blurry images as they can distract from your message.

Use images sparingly: While images can be a powerful tool, it is important not to overuse them. Too many images can distract from your content and make it harder for readers to focus.

Choose appropriate file formats: Different image file formats are better suited for different uses. For example, JPEG is a good choice for photographs, while PNG is better for graphics with transparent backgrounds.

Use alt text: Alt text is a description of an image that is displayed when the image cannot be shown. It is important to include alt text as it can help to improve the accessibility of your content and boost your SEO.

Experiment with other visual elements: In addition to images, there are many other visual elements you can use to enhance your content. These may include videos, infographics, charts, and diagrams.

By using visual elements effectively, you can add interest and depth to your content and make it more engaging for your audience.

The Power of Storytelling in Content Writing

Storytelling is a powerful tool for content writers as it can help to engage and connect with readers in a way that simply presenting information cannot. By incorporating elements of storytelling into your content, you can make it more memorable and impactful for your audience. Here are a few tips for using storytelling in your content writing:

Use characters: Characters are an essential element of storytelling and can help to bring your content to life. Whether you are writing about real people or fictional characters, they can help to make your content more relatable and engaging.

Include a plot: A plot is the series of events that make up a story. By including a plot in your content, you can create a sense of momentum and keep your readers interested.

Use descriptive language: Descriptive language can help to bring your story to life and transport your readers to the world you are describing. Use sensory details to help your readers feel like they are experiencing your story firsthand.

Use dialogue: Dialogue is a great way to add depth and authenticity to your story. It can also help to reveal the character and move the plot forward.

Edit and revise: As with any piece of writing, it is important to edit and revise your story to ensure that it is clear, concise, and engaging. This may involve cutting unnecessary details, reordering events, or revising your dialogue.

Storytelling can be a powerful tool for content writers. By incorporating elements of storytelling into your content, you can create engaging and memorable pieces that connect with your readers on a deeper level.

Using Data and Statistics to Enhance Your Writing:
Incorporating data and statistics into your content can add credibility, depth, and interest to your writing. However, it is important to use this information effectively in order to enhance, rather than distract from, your message. Here are a few tips for using data and statistics effectively in your writing:

Choose relevant and reliable sources: It is important to use data and statistics from reputable sources that are relevant to your topic. This will help to ensure the accuracy and reliability of your information.

Use data and statistics sparingly: While data and statistics can be powerful tools, it is important not to overuse them. Too much information can be overwhelming and distract from your main message.

Use charts and graphs to visualize data: Visual aids like charts and graphs can help to make data and statistics more accessible and easier to understand. Choose the right type of chart or graph for the data you are presenting and be sure to label it clearly.

Explain the context of the data: It is important to provide context for the data and statistics you are presenting. This may include explaining the source of the data, the time period it covers, and how it relates to your topic.

Cite your sources: Be sure to properly cite your sources for any data or statistics you include in your writing. This will help to establish your credibility and allow readers to verify the information for them.

By using data and statistics effectively, you can enhance your writing and add depth and credibility to your content.

SEO Best Practices for Content Writers
As a content writer, it is important to consider search engine optimization (SEO)

in order to make your content more discoverable and improve its ranking in search results. Here are a few SEO best practices for content writers:

Use relevant keywords: Choose keywords that are relevant to your content and the terms your audience is likely to search for. Incorporate these keywords naturally into your content and use them in your headlines, subheadings, and alt text for images.

Use Meta titles and descriptions: Meta titles and descriptions are tags that appear in search results and help to give readers an idea of what your content is about. These tags should be descriptive and include relevant keywords.

Use header tags: Header tags (H1, H2, etc.) help to indicate the hierarchy of your content and give search engines an idea of the structure and importance of your content. Use header tags to break up your content and make it easier for readers to scan and understand.

Use internal and external links: Linking to other relevant and reputable sources can help to improve the credibility and authority of your content. It is also a good idea to use internal links to direct readers to other relevant content on your site.

Optimize images and videos: Use descriptive file names and alt text for images and videos to help search engines understand the content of these elements. This can also improve the accessibility of your content for users who rely on screen readers.

By following these SEO best practices, you can improve the discoverability and ranking of your content and reach a wider audience.

Creating Engaging Social Media Posts
Social media is an important platform for content writers as it allows you to share your content with a wider audience and engage with your readers. Here are a few tips for creating engaging social media posts:

Use attention-grabbing headlines: Just like with any piece of writing, it is important to use a compelling headline for your social media posts. Keep it short and sweet and use strong action verbs to grab your readers' attention.

Use visuals: Social media is a visual medium, so be sure to use images, videos, and other visual elements in your posts. Choose high-quality, relevant visuals that will grab your readers' attention and enhance your message.

Use hash tags: Hash tags are a great way to reach a wider audience and join the conversation on social media. Choose relevant hash tags and use them sparingly to avoid overwhelming your readers.

Engage with your followers: Social media is all about engagement, so be sure to respond to comments and questions from your followers. This can help to build a community around your content and foster a sense of connection with your readers.

Experiment with different types of content: Social media is a versatile platform, so don't be afraid to experiment with different types of content. This may include text-based posts, images, videos, polls, and more.

By following these tips, you can create engaging social media posts that connect with your audience and drive traffic to your content.

Writing for Email Marketing

Email marketing is a powerful tool for content writers as it allows you to directly reach and engage with your audience. Here are a few tips for writing effective emails for marketing purposes:

Use a compelling subject line: The subject line of your email is the first thing your readers will see, so it is important to make it attention-grabbing. Use strong action verbs and make it clear what the email is about.

Keep it short and sweet: Emails should be concise and to the point. Avoid using long blocks of text and break up your content into easily digestible chunks.

Use formatting and layout effectively: Formatting and layout can help to make your emails more visually appealing and easier to read. Use headings, bullet points, and white space to break up your content and make it easier to scan.

Use images and other visual elements: Visual elements can help to make your emails more engaging and memorable. Choose high-quality, relevant images and use them sparingly to avoid overwhelming your readers.

Include a call to action: Your emails should have a clear purpose, whether it is to drive traffic to your website, encourage readers to make a purchase, or sign up for a newsletter. Be sure to include a clear call to action that tells your readers what you want them to do next.

By following these tips, you can create effective email marketing campaigns that engage and convert your audience.

Crafting Compelling Product Descriptions
As a content writer, you may be called upon to write product descriptions for e-commerce websites or marketing materials. Here are a few tips for crafting compelling product descriptions:

Use descriptive language: Product descriptions should provide detailed information about the product and its features. Use descriptive language to bring the product to life and help customers visualize it.

Focus on the benefits: While it is important to list the features of the product, it is also crucial to highlight the benefits to the customer. How will the product solve a problem or improve their life?

Use bullet points: Bullet points are a great way to present information in a clear and concise manner. Use them to highlight key features and benefits of the product.

Include customer testimonials: Including customer, testimonials can help to build credibility and establish trust with potential buyers. Choose testimonials that highlight the benefits of the product and how it has improved the customer's life.

Edit and revise: As with any piece of writing, it is important to edit and revise your product descriptions to ensure that they are clear, concise, and free of errors.

By following these tips, you can craft compelling product descriptions that effectively sell the product to your audience.

The Role of Editing in the Writing Process
Editing is an essential step in the writing process as it helps to ensure that your

content is clear, accurate, and free of errors. Here are a few tips for effective editing:

Set aside time for editing: Make sure to allow sufficient time for the editing process. It is often helpful to take a break from your writing and come back to it with fresh eyes.

Use editing tools: There are many tools available to help with the editing process, such as grammar and spell checkers, style guides, and online dictionaries. These tools can help to identify errors and ensure that your content is polished and professional.

Review the content for clarity and concision: During the editing process, it is important to review your content for clarity and concision. Cut unnecessary words and phrases and rephrase awkward sentences to make your content more readable and easy to understand.

Check for accuracy: Editing is also an opportunity to check your content for accuracy. Verify facts and figures, and ensure that your content is consistent with any sources you have used.

Have someone else review your work: It can be helpful to have someone else review your work to catch errors or suggest improvements. This may be a colleague, friend, or professional editor.

Editing is an important step in the writing process that should not be overlooked. By following these tips, you can create polished and professional content that is clear and accurate.

Developing a Content Marketing Strategy
A content marketing strategy is a plan for creating and distributing valuable, relevant, and consistent content to attract and retain a clearly defined audience. Here are a few steps to follow when developing a content marketing strategy:

Define your target audience: The first step in developing a content marketing strategy is to identify your target audience. Consider factors such as demographics, interests, and pain points to get a clear picture of who you are trying to reach.

Set your goals: Next, you will need to define your goals for your content marketing efforts. These goals may include increasing brand awareness, generating leads, or driving sales.

Identify your content pillars: Content pillars are the main topics or themes that your content will revolve around. Identify a few broad topics that are relevant to your target audience and will help you achieve your goals.

Create a content calendar: A content calendar is a schedule of the content you plan to create and publish. It can help you to plan ahead, stay organized, and ensure that you are consistently publishing new content.

Promote your content: Once you have created your content, it is important to promote it to your target audience. This may involve sharing it on social media, sending newsletters, or utilizing paid advertising.

By following these steps, you can develop a comprehensive content marketing strategy that helps you to achieve your goals and connect with your target audience.

Measuring the Success of Your Content

Measuring the success of your content is an important step in understanding what is working and what areas may need improvement. Here are a few metrics you may want to consider when evaluating the success of your content:

Traffic: One way to measure the success of your content is to track the number of visitors to your site. This can help you to see how your content is performing and whether it is driving traffic to your site.

Engagement: Engagement metrics, such as likes, comments, and shares, can help you to gauge the level of interest and interaction your content is generating.

Conversion rates: Conversion rates refer to the percentage of visitors who take a desired action, such as making a purchase or signing up for a newsletter. Tracking conversion rates can help you to see how effective your content is at achieving your goals.

Bounce rate: Bounce rate refers to the percentage of visitors who leave your site after viewing only one page. A high bounce rate may indicate that your content is not engaging or relevant to your audience.

Time on page: Tracking the amount of time visitors spend on your site can help you to understand how engaging and useful your content is.

By tracking these metrics, you can get a better understanding of the success of your content and identify areas for improvement.

Repurposing Your Content for Multiple Channels
Repurposing your content for multiple channels can help to maximize its reach and value. Here are a few tips for repurposing your content for different channels:

Identify the core message: The first step in repurposing your content is to identify the core message or theme that you want to convey. This will help you to focus your efforts and ensure that your content stays consistent across different channels.

Adapt the format: Different channels may require different formats for your content. For example, what works on a blog may not work as well on social media or in an email newsletter. Adapt the format of your content to fit the specific channel you are using.

Use different headlines: Headlines are crucial for grabbing the attention of your audience. Consider using different headlines for different channels to appeal to specific audiences and encourage them to click through to your content.

Include relevant hashtags: Hashtags can help to increase the reach of your content on social media. Use relevant hashtags that are specific to the channel you are using.

Link to your original content: When repurposing your content, be sure to include links to the original source. This will help to drive traffic back to your site and increase the visibility of your content.

By repurposing your content for multiple channels, you can reach a wider audience and maximize the value of your content.

Collaborating with Other Writers and Editors

As a content writer, you may find yourself working with other writers and editors as part of a team. Here are a few tips for effective collaboration:

Establish clear communication channels: It is important to establish clear communication channels to ensure that everyone is on the same page. This may involve using project management tools, setting up regular check-ins, or using video conferencing software.

Set clear roles and responsibilities: Clearly defining roles and responsibilities can help to prevent confusion and ensure that everyone is aware of their tasks and deadlines.

Use revision tracking tools: Revision tracking tools, such as those found in word processing software, can be helpful for keeping track of changes and feedback from other writers and editors.

Seek feedback and be open to revisions: Collaboration often involves seeking feedback and making revisions based on that feedback. Be open to suggestions and consider them carefully to improve your content.

Respect each other's time and workload: Collaboration requires a team effort and it is important to respect each other's time and workload. Be considerate of others' schedules and deadlines, and communicate any changes or issues in a timely manner.

By following these tips, you can effectively collaborate with other writers and editors and create high-quality content as a team.

Writing for International Audiences
Writing for an international audience requires considering cultural differences and adapting your content to make it more accessible and relevant to your readers. Here are a few tips for writing for international audiences:

Research your target audience: It is important to research your target audience and understand their cultural differences and preferences. This may include considering factors such as language, customs, and values.

Use plain language: To make your content more accessible to a wider audience, it is important to use plain language that is easy to understand. Avoid jargon and technical terms, and consider using a simpler vocabulary.

Consider language and translation issues: If you are writing in a language that is not your native tongue, it is important to be aware of language and translation issues. Consider hiring a translator or working with a language expert to ensure that your content is accurate and effectively communicates your message.

Adapt your content to local customs and values: Be mindful of local customs and values when writing for an international audience. This may involve adjusting your tone, avoiding sensitive topics, and considering cultural differences in humor and sarcasm.

Use local examples and references: Using local examples and references can help to make your content more relatable and relevant to your international audience. This may include incorporating local news, cultural events, and famous figures.

By following these tips, you can effectively write for an international audience and create content .

The Ethics of Content Writing

As a content writer, it is important to be aware of the ethical considerations involved in creating and distributing content. Here are a few tips for ethical content writing:

Respect copyright laws: It is important to respect copyright laws and only use content that you have the rights to use. This may include obtaining permission to use images, quotes, or other materials that are not in the public domain.

Fact-check your information: It is crucial to fact-check your information to ensure that it is accurate and reliable. Use credible sources and double-check your facts to avoid spreading misinformation.

Avoid plagiarism: Plagiarism is the act of using someone else's work or ideas without proper attribution. It is important to properly cite your sources and give credit to others for their work to avoid plagiarism.

Be transparent: It is important to be transparent about your sources and any potential conflicts of interest. Disclose any sponsored content or partnerships and be honest about the purpose of your content.

Consider the impact of your content: As a content writer, you have the power to influence your readers. Be mindful of the impact of your content and consider the consequences of your words and actions.

By following these ethical guidelines, you can create content that is responsible, trustworthy, and respectful of others.

Navigating Legal Issues in Content Writing

As a content writer, it is important to be aware of the legal considerations involved in creating and distributing content. Here are a few tips for navigating legal issues in content writing:

Respect copyright laws: It is important to respect copyright laws and only use content that you have the rights to use. This may include obtaining permission to use images, quotes, or other materials that are not in the public domain.

Use caution when discussing sensitive topics: When writing about sensitive topics such as politics, religion, or controversial issues, it is important to be careful not to defame or libel anyone. Avoid making false or defamatory statements and be mindful of the potential consequences of your words.

Protect confidential information: If you have access to confidential information, it is important to protect it and only use it in accordance with any agreements or non-disclosure agreements you may have signed.

Consider the terms of use for platforms and services: When using platforms or services to distribute your content, be sure to review the terms of use and ensure that you are in compliance.

Obtain legal review when necessary: If you are unsure about the legal implications of your content, it may be necessary to seek legal review or seek advice from a legal professional.

By following these guidelines, you can navigate legal issues in content writing and create content that is compliant with relevant laws and regulations.

Writing for Niche Markets
Writing for niche markets requires a deep understanding of the needs and interests of a specific group of readers. Here are a few tips for writing for niche markets:

Research your target audience: It is important to thoroughly research your target audience and understand their needs, interests, and pain points. This may involve conducting surveys, focus groups, or interviews to gather insights.

Use language and terminology specific to the niche: To effectively communicate with your target audience, it is important to use language and terminology that is specific to their niche. This may require becoming familiar with industry-specific terms and concepts.

Address the unique challenges and concerns of the niche: Niche markets often have unique challenges and concerns that are specific to their industry or interests. Be sure to address these issues in your content and provide solutions or insights that are relevant to your audience.

Utilize niche-specific platforms and communities: Niche markets often have their own platforms and communities where you can share your content and engage with your target audience. Utilize these channels to reach your audience and build your credibility within the niche.

Collaborate with experts and influencers: Collaborating with experts and influencers in your niche can help to add credibility to your content and expose it to a wider audience. Consider reaching out to these individuals for guest posts, interviews, or collaborations.

By following these tips, you can effectively write for niche markets and create content that resonates with and serves your target audience.

The Future of Content Writing

The field of content writing is constantly evolving as new technologies and platforms emerge. Here are a few trends that are shaping the future of content writing:

The rise of artificial intelligence and machine learning: Artificial intelligence (AI) and machine learning are being used to automate and enhance various aspects of content creation, such as generating ideas, writing, and editing. It is important for content writers to stay up-to-date on these technologies and consider how they may impact their work.

The increasing importance of video content: Video content is becoming increasingly popular and is expected to continue to grow in the coming years. Content writers may need to adapt their skills to include video production and scripting in order to meet the demand for this type of content.

The growth of voice search and voice assistants: The use of voice search and voice assistants is on the rise, and it is expected that this trend will continue in the future. Content writers will need to optimize their content for voice search and consider how it will be consumed through voice assistants.

The need for personalization: As the amount of available content continues to grow, it is becoming increasingly important to personalize content in order to stand out and engage readers. Content writers will need to consider how to tailor their content to specific audiences and use data to inform their writing.

By staying up-to-date on these trends and adapting their skills accordingly, content writers can position themselves for success in the future.

Mastering Different Writing Styles
As a content writer, it is important to be able to adapt your writing style to different situations and audiences. Here are a few tips for mastering different writing styles:

Understand the purpose of your writing: The purpose of your writing will often dictate the style you should use. For example, if you are writing a technical manual, you will likely use a different style than if you are writing a creative piece of fiction.

Know your audience: The audience you are writing for will also influence your writing style. Consider the age, education level, and interests of your readers and adjust your style accordingly.

Use the appropriate tone: The tone of your writing should match the purpose and audience of your content. For example, a formal tone may be more appropriate for a legal document, while a more casual tone may be suitable for a blog post.

Vary your sentence structure: Varying your sentence structure can help to keep your writing interesting and engaging. Mix up your use of short and long sentences, and consider using rhetorical devices such as repetition or parallelism for emphasis.

Edit and proofread: It is important to edit and proofread your writing to ensure that it is clear, concise, and free of errors. This will help to improve the overall quality of your writing and make it more effective.

By mastering different writing styles, you can effectively adapt your writing to different situations and audiences and create content that is engaging and effective.

Adapting Your Writing for Different Formats

As a content writer, you may be called upon to write for different formats, such as blog posts, articles, social media posts, and email newsletters. Here are a few tips for adapting your writing for different formats:

Understand the purpose and audience of the format: The purpose and audience of the format you are writing for will often dictate the style and content of your writing. Be sure to consider these factors when adapting your writing for different formats.

Use appropriate tone and language: The tone and language you use should match the format and audience of your content. For example, a more casual and conversational tone may be suitable for social media posts, while a more formal tone may be appropriate for articles or reports.

Consider the length and structure of the format: Different formats will have different length and structure requirements. For example, a blog post may be longer and more in-depth than a social media post, while an email newsletter may have a specific layout and design to consider.

Use visuals and formatting: Visuals and formatting can help to make your content more engaging and appealing. Consider using images, videos, and formatting options such as headings and bullet points to enhance the readability and impact of your writing.

By adapting your writing to different formats, you can effectively create content that is relevant and engaging for your audience.

Overcoming Writer's Block
Writer's block is a common challenge that many writers face at some point in their careers. Here are a few tips for overcoming writer's block:

Take breaks: Sometimes taking a break from writing can help to clear your mind and allow you to approach your work with a fresh perspective. Consider stepping away from your work for a short period of time and returning to it later.

Change your environment: Changing your environment can help to stimulate your creativity and get your ideas flowing. Consider working in a different location or trying a new writing spot.

Warm up with writing exercises: Writing exercises can help to get your creative juices flowing and overcome writer's block. Try free writing, where you write as quickly as possible without worrying about grammar or structure, or try writing prompts to spark your creativity.

Get organized: Sometimes writer's block can be caused by a lack of organization or structure. Consider creating an outline or a plan for your writing to help you stay focused and on track.

Seek feedback: Getting feedback from others can help to provide new ideas and perspectives, and may help to overcome writer's block. Consider sharing your work with a writing group or a trusted colleague for feedback and suggestions.

By following these tips, you can overcome writer's block and get back to creating high-quality content.

The Business of Freelance Writing
Freelance writing can be a rewarding and lucrative career, but it also involves running your own business. Here are a few tips for managing the business side of freelance writing:

Define your niche: Specializing in a particular niche can help to differentiate you from other writers and make you more attractive to potential clients. Consider your strengths, interests, and experience, and define your niche accordingly.

Create a portfolio: A portfolio is a collection of your writing samples that showcases your skills and experience. It is important to regularly update your portfolio with your best work and include a diverse range of samples.

Develop a marketing plan: Marketing yourself is crucial for attracting new clients and building your freelance writing business. Consider creating a website, networking with potential clients, and utilizing social media and online platforms to promote your services.

Set clear terms and expectations: Clearly communicating your terms and expectations to clients can help to prevent misunderstandings and ensure that you are paid fairly for your work. Consider creating a contract or proposal outlining your rates, deadlines, and deliverables.

Stay organized: Managing multiple clients and projects can be challenging, so it is important to stay organized and keep track of your tasks and deadlines. Consider using a project management tool or creating a system to help you stay on top of your workload.

By following these tips, you can effectively manage the business side of freelance writing and build a successful and sustainable career.

Managing Your Online Presence as a Writer

As a writer, your online presence can be a powerful tool for attracting clients, building your reputation, and showcasing your work. Here are a few tips for managing your online presence as a writer:

Create a professional website: A website is a great way to showcase your writing samples, bio, and services. Consider investing in a professional website design and be sure to include relevant information about your writing background and experience.

Use social media to your advantage: Social media can be a powerful tool for promoting your writing and engaging with potential clients. Consider setting up accounts on relevant platforms and sharing your work, insights, and updates regularly.

Network with other writers and industry professionals: Networking with other writers and industry professionals can help to build your reputation and expose you to potential clients. Consider joining writing groups or attending industry events to make connections.

Protect your online reputation: Your online reputation is important, so it is important to be mindful of what you post online and how you present yourself. Be professional and respectful in your online interactions and consider the long-term impact of your online presence.

Regularly update your online profiles and portfolio: It is important to regularly update your online profiles and portfolio to showcase your current work and accomplishments. Consider adding new writing samples and updates on a regular basis to keep your online presence current and relevant.

By following these tips, you can effectively manage your online presence as a writer and use it to your advantage.

Networking and Building Your Professional Network

Networking and building a professional network can be valuable for writers in terms of finding new clients, learning about opportunities, and getting advice and support. Here are a few tips for networking and building your professional network:

Attend industry events: Industry events and conferences can be a great way to meet other writers and industry professionals and learn about new opportunities. Consider attending events that are relevant to your niche and make an effort to connect with others.

Join writing groups and organizations: Joining writing groups and organizations can help you to connect with other writers and learn about industry best practices. Consider joining local or online groups or joining a professional organization such as the American Society of Journalists and Authors.

Utilize social media: Social media platforms can be a powerful tool for networking and connecting with other writers and industry professionals. Consider following relevant accounts and participating in online writing groups and communities.

Reach out to other writers for collaborations or advice: Don't be afraid to reach out to other writers for collaborations or advice. Many writers are happy to share their experience and knowledge and may be open to working with you on a project or offering guidance.

Cultivate relationships: Building relationships with other writers and industry professionals takes time and effort, but it can be valuable in the long run. Consider maintaining regular contact with your network and offering your help and support when appropriate.

By following these tips, you can effectively network and build a professional network that can benefit your writing career.

Continuing Your Education as a Writer

As a writer, it is important to continually learn and grow in order to stay current and improve your skills. Here are a few tips for continuing your education as a writer:

Read widely: Reading is a great way to expose yourself to different writing styles and ideas, and can help to improve your own writing skills. Consider reading a variety of genres and styles and pay attention to the techniques and strategies used by the authors.

Take writing courses and workshops: Taking writing courses and workshops can help you to learn new skills and techniques and receive feedback on your work. Consider looking for local classes or online options that fit your needs and schedule.

Join a writing group: Joining a writing group can provide a supportive and constructive environment for learning and improving your writing. Consider finding a local writing group or joining an online community to connect with other writers and receive feedback on your work.

Practice regularly: The best way to improve your writing skills is to practice regularly. Set aside time to write every day or on a regular basis and challenge yourself to try new techniques and styles.

Stay current: Keeping up with industry trends and developments can help you to stay current and relevant as a writer. Consider subscribing to writing-related newsletters or following industry blogs and publications to stay informed.

By following these tips, you can continue your education as a writer and improve your skills over time.

Introduction: The Importance of Strong Titles in Content Marketing
Tip 1: Clearly and Concisely Communicate the Topic of Your Article
Tip 2: Incorporate Keywords for SEO Benefits

The Importance of Strong Titles in Content Marketing:

A strong title is crucial for successful content marketing. It is the first thing that a reader sees and can be the deciding factor in whether or not they choose to read on. A strong title should be attention-grabbing, informative, and accurately reflect the content of the piece.

Here are a few reasons why strong titles are important in content marketing:

A strong title can increase click-through rates: And a well-written title can entice readers to click on a link and read more. This is especially important for content that is being shared on social media or in email newsletters, where the title is often

the only thing a reader sees before deciding to click.

A strong title can improve search engine optimization (SEO): A title that accurately reflects the content of an article and includes relevant keywords can improve the article's ranking on search engines. This can lead to more organic traffic to the website and increase the visibility of the content.

A strong title can establish credibility: A clear and informative title can establish the writer as a thought leader in their industry and give readers confidence in the content they are about to read.

In summary, strong titles are essential for successful content marketing. They can increase click-through rates, improve SEO, and establish credibility with readers.

Clearly and Concisely Communicate the Topic of Your Article:
It is important to clearly and concisely communicate the topic of your article in order to grab the reader's attention and keep them engaged. Here are a few tips for effectively communicating the topic of your article:

Use a clear and concise title: The title of your article should accurately reflect the content and give readers a good idea of what they can expect to read. Avoid using overly complex or jargon-heavy language, as this can be off-putting to readers.

Use subheadings: Subheadings can help to break up the text and make it easier for readers to quickly scan the article and understand its main points. Use descriptive subheadings that clearly communicate the topic of each section.

Use bullet points: Bullet points are a great way to present information in a clear and concise manner. They can help to break up large blocks of text and make it easier for readers to quickly digest the information.

Use images and graphics: Visual elements such as images and graphics can help to communicate complex concepts and make the article more engaging for readers.

By following these tips, you can help to clearly and concisely communicate the topic of your article and keep readers engaged from start to finish.

Incorporate Keywords for SEO Benefits
Incorporating keywords into your content can have numerous benefits for search engine optimization (SEO). Keywords are words or phrases that are relevant to the content of your website and that people are likely to search for when looking for information online. By including these keywords in your content, you can help search engines understand what your website is about and improve its ranking in search results.

Here are a few tips for incorporating keywords into your content for SEO benefits:

Use keywords in your titles and headings: Titles and headings are important for both readers and search engines, so it's a good idea to include relevant keywords in these areas.

Use keywords in the body of your content: Including keywords naturally in the body of your content will help search engines understand the topic of your website and improve its ranking. However, be sure to use keywords sparingly and in a way that reads naturally for readers.

Use long-tail keywords: Long-tail keywords are longer, more specific phrases that are less competitive and can drive targeted traffic to your website.

Use variations of your keywords: Don't just use the same keyword over and over again. Mix it up with variations and synonyms to avoid keyword stuffing and make your content more readable.

By following these tips and incorporating relevant keywords into your content, you can help improve your website's ranking on search engines and drive more organic traffic to your site.

Use Power Words to Grab Attention and Emotionally Connect with Readers
Power words are words that elicit an emotional response and can help to grab the attention of readers. These words are often used in headlines and call to action to persuade and motivate readers to take a desired action.

Here are a few examples of powerful words:

Free: This is a powerful word that can grab the attention of anyone looking for a good deal.

New: This word can create a sense of excitement and curiosity, as it implies that something is innovative or up-to-date.

You: This word can create a sense of personalization and make readers feel like the content is directly relevant to them.

Limited time: This phrase creates a sense of urgency and can motivate readers to take action before it's too late.

Easy: This word can appeal to readers who are looking for a quick and simple solution to their problem.

By using powerful words in your content, you can grab the attention of readers and emotionally connect with them, increasing the chances that they will take the desired action.

Consider the Length and Formatting of Your Title
The length and formatting of your title can have a big impact on how effective it is at grabbing the attention of readers and

accurately communicating the content of your article. Here are a few things to consider when crafting a title:

Length: A title that is too long may be truncated in search results or social media feeds, making it difficult for readers to understand the content of the article. On the other hand, a title that is too short may not provide enough context for readers to know what to expect from the article. Aim for a title that is around 50-60 characters in length.

Formatting: The use of capitalization, bold or italicized text, and punctuation can all affect the readability and impact of a title. Use formatting sparingly and in a way that helps to emphasize the most important words.

Keywords: Be sure to include relevant keywords in your title, as this can help with search engine optimization (SEO) and improve the visibility of your content.

By considering the length and formatting of your title, you can create a title that is effective at grabbing the attention of readers and accurately communicating the content of your article.

Test and Tweak Your Titles for Maximum Impact

Testing and tweaking your titles can help to ensure that they are as effective as possible at grabbing the attention of readers and accurately communicating the content of your article. Here are a few tips for testing and tweaking your titles:

Test different versions: Create a few different versions of your title and test them to see which one performs the best. This can be done by sharing the titles on social media or email newsletters and tracking the click-through rates.

Include a strong verb: A strong verb can help to convey the action or purpose of the article and make the title more attention-grabbing.

Use numbers: Titles that include numbers can be more eye-catching and provide a clear idea of the content of the article.

Use negative words sparingly: While negative words can be attention-grabbing, they can also be off-putting to readers. Use them sparingly and in a way that accurately reflects the content of the article.

By testing and tweaking your titles, you can improve their effectiveness and increase the chances that readers will click on and read your content.

The Role of Titles in Driving Traffic and Engagement

The role of titles in driving traffic and engagement is significant. A title is the first thing that a reader sees and it can either entice them to click and read further or cause them to move on.

A good title should be descriptive, accurate, and attention-grabbing. It should clearly convey the content and theme of the article and be relevant to the target audience. It should also be unique and stand out in a sea of competing titles.

Titles that are too long or vague may not be effective in driving traffic and engagement. Similarly, titles that are overly sensational or clickbaity may attract clicks initially, but may not lead to long-term engagement or trust from the readers.

In addition to being informative and compelling, it is also important for the title to be SEO-friendly. This means including relevant keywords and phrases that people may be searching for. This can help improve the visibility and ranking of the article in search engine results, which can lead to more traffic and engagement.

Overall, the role of titles in driving traffic and engagement is crucial. They serve as the gateway to the content and can make a big impact on the success of an article.

Utilize Sub headers to Further Clarify and Organize Your Content

Sub headers, also known as subheadings or section headings, are a useful tool for clarifying and organizing content. They break up long blocks of text and make it easier for readers to scan and understand the main points of an article.

Sub headers should be used to summarize or highlight the key takeaways of each section of the content. They should be descriptive and accurately reflect the content that follows. They should also be written in a way that is easy to understand and adds value to the reader.

In addition to improving the readability of content, sub headers can also help with SEO. Including relevant keywords and phrases in sub headers, it can help improve the visibility and ranking of the article in search engine results.

To effectively utilize sub headers, it is important to keep them short and to the point. They should not be too long or wordy, as this can detract from their effectiveness. It is also important to use sub headers consistently and to appropriately divide the content into sections that are logical and coherent.

In summary, sub headers are a useful tool for clarifying and organizing content and can help improve the readability and SEO of an article. Utilizing sub headers effectively can help drive traffic and engagement by making it easier for readers to understand and navigate the content.

Attracting words, also known as persuasive or power words, are words that have the ability to influence the emotions and actions of readers. They can be used to grab the attention of readers and motivate them to take a certain action, such as visiting a website, signing up for a newsletter, or making a purchase. Here are some examples of attractive words that content writers can use to make their writing more engaging and effective:

"Free" - This is a powerful word that can be used to entice people to take action, by offering something of value at no cost

"New" - People are always on the lookout for something new, so use this word to make your product or service sound exciting and innovative

"Proven" - This word implies that your product or service has been tested and is guaranteed to work, which can help build trust with potential customers

"Exclusive" - This word implies that the content or offer is only available to a select group of people, which can create a sense of scarcity and exclusivity

"Easy" - This word can be used to make your product or service sound simple and hassle-free

"Save" - This word implies that the customer will be getting a good deal or saving money, which can be a powerful motivator for people to take action

"Guaranteed" - this word will help to assure the readers about the credibility and reliability of your product or service.

"You/Your" - this word will help in making the readers feel more connected and personalized.
"Discover" - this word creates a sense of adventure and curiosity, leading to more engagement with the content
Using these words and phrases in headlines, call-to-action buttons, headlines, and other key parts of your content can make it more appealing to your audience and encourage them to take action.

Conclusion

Being a content writer is a challenging but rewarding career that requires a combination of writing skills, creativity, research abilities, and an understanding of marketing. A content writer is responsible for creating various forms of written content such as articles, blog posts, social media updates, product descriptions, and other types of marketing materials.

To be a successful content writer, it's important to have a strong grasp of grammar and language, the ability to write in various styles and formats, and an understanding of search engine optimization (SEO) principles to help increase the visibility of the content. Additionally, it's important to stay current on industry trends and be able to research and write about a variety of topics. Creating high-quality, engaging, and relevant content that resonates with the target audience is key. It's important to understand the audience's needs, interests, and pain points and create content that provides value and addresses them. Additionally, it's important to have a strong understanding of marketing principles, so that the content can be used to effectively promote products, services, or ideas.Working as a content writer also involves working with other team members such as editors, designers, and marketers to ensure that the content aligns with the overall marketing strategy. A good Content writer should be able to collaborate effectively and deliver content in timely manners.

In conclusion, a content writer is a professional who is responsible for creating various forms of written content to attract, engage and convert the target audience. A successful content writer should have strong writing and research skills, be creative, and have an understanding of marketing and SEO. By creating high-quality and relevant content, understanding the target audience, and working effectively with a team, a content writer can help to generate leads and conversions, establish a company or brand as an authority in the industry and create an impactful online presence.

www.ingramcontent.com/pod-product-compliance
Lightning Source LLC
LaVergne TN
LVHW051333050326
832903LV00031B/3522